EDWARD LEAR
AND THE
PUSSYCAT

For
Philip and Phyllis,
Wilma,
Edward, Robert, and Thomas

First published 2019 by
The British Library
96 Euston Road
London NW1 2DB

Cataloguing in Publication Data
A catalogue record for this publication is available
from The British Library

ISBN 978 0 7123 5244 4

Typeset by Lee-May Lim
Cover design by Will Webb
Printed and bound by Gutenberg Press, Malta

EDWARD LEAR
AND THE
PUSSYCAT

FAMOUS WRITERS AND THEIR PETS

ALEX JOHNSON

CONTENTS

INTRODUCTION

From white whales to black horses, and rabbits in jackets to polar bears in armour, animals have always inspired writers. The once and future king changes into a hawk. The king of the elephants wears a bright green suit. Pigs become revolutionaries.

And of course as pets, they also make ideal companions. Pets force their writer-owners outside to get some exercise where their humans are also likely to meet other humans, they are (nearly) always loyal, and they provide companionship in what is often a very lonely working existence. They also offer practical services too, although sometimes, of course, they also eat first drafts and bite visitors. But even then they are loved. Usually.

Here then is an alphabetical walk through the world's favourite writers and the much loved pets who enriched their lives, sat on their keyboards, and slept in their beds, cats and dogs, snails and ravens, more peacocks than you would expect, wombats, bears, guinea pigs, budgerigars, monkeys, and one potto.

A

IS FOR ...

ADORNO

Argentinian novelist Julio Cortázar (1914–1984), author of *Bestiario* (1951) and *Hopscotch* (1963) among others, named his black cat Theodor W. Adorno after the German philosopher and avant-garde pianist of the same name whom Cortázar admired. Theodor (the cat) features regularly in Cortázar's collection of essays *Around the Day in Eighty Worlds* (1967), being fed, playing with the writer, and at one point suddenly freezing and staring at what appeared to be empty space as if he had seen a ghost.

ADVICE

Science-fiction writer Ray Bradbury and his wife Marguerite owned nearly two dozen cats in the 1950s, though their numbers dropped over the following decades. In his book *Zen in the Art of Writing* (1990), he talked about the key to writing: 'As soon as things get difficult, I walk away. That's the great secret of creativity. You treat ideas like cats: you make them follow you.'

AIKEN

In her introduction to *Gobbolino the Witch's Cat* by Ursula Moray Williams, novelist Joan Aiken (1924–2004) reveals that she had several cats including January (who could open door latches), Gracchus (an epileptic tabby who belonged to her sister), Hamlet (who grew very jealous of Gracchus's daily treatment of pills), and Darwin (who liked to lie on her neck). Her other cats included the very sociable Taffy who, while disliking dogs intensely, regularly brought cat friends into the house, including Whisky from a nearby pub who used to wash herself in Aiken's kitchen sink, and Tetanus from the local hairdresser's who slept on top of the china cupboard. Taffy and his friends used to play tag outside in the garden while Aiken wrote inside the house.

ARNOLD

Poet and critic Matthew Arnold (1822–1888) had a pet Dachshund, Geist, for four years. When Geist died, Arnold wrote a poem in 1881 called 'Geist's Grave' about how much fun and love his devoted dog had squeezed into their short time together, including the lines:

> We stroke thy broad brown paws again,
> We bid thee to thy vacant chair,
> We greet thee by the window-pane,
> We hear thy scuffle on the stair.

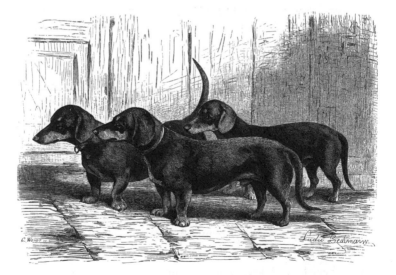

AUDEN

'Cats can be very funny, and have the oddest ways of showing they're glad to see you. Rudimace always peed in our shoes.'
W.H. Auden, poet and owner of Rudimace

W.H. Auden (1907–1973) also had a cat called Pangur whom he named after the cat in the ninth-century Irish poem 'Pangur Bán'. His translation of it, later set to music by Samuel Barber as part of his song cycle 'Hermit Songs' (1953), starts:

> Pangur, white Pangur, How happy we are
> Alone together, scholar and cat.

AUGUSTUS

V.S. Naipaul (1932–2018), winner of the Nobel Prize in Literature in 2001, became very attached to his black and white cat Augustus, regularly getting up in the middle of the night to give him a drink of water. When he and his wife Nadira travelled, they limited their time away because their absence unsettled Augustus, and they paid for two cat-sitters to keep him happy.

After Augustus died following a kick to the head by a cow, Naipaul told *The New Republic*: 'It was calamitous for me. I feel a deep, deep grief… I think of Augustus. He was the sum of my experiences. He had taken on my outlook, my way of living.' Naipaul had assumed Augustus would outlive him and included him in his will. He placed a notice in the *Times* announcing his death.

B

IS FOR ...

BARON

One of the most remarkable examples of pets' homing instincts is that of Baron, the Poodle who belonged to novelist Victor Hugo (1802–1885). Historian Rupert Willoughby has recounted how Hugo gave Baron to his great, great grandfather the Marquis de Faletans in 1877 when he noticed how much the Marquis was admiring him during a visit to his apartment in Paris. A week later, the Marquis went on a trip to his family estate in Russia, 320 kilometres (200 miles) south of Moscow. Several months later, in December, he told Hugo in a letter that Baron had gone missing, presumed dead. So Hugo was surprised to be told on Christmas Day by his cook that Baron had turned up at their front door, hungry and barking loudly, having made the 3,200-kilometre (2,000-mile) trip back by himself.

BASKET

Writer and literary salon hostess Gertrude Stein (1874–1946) and her partner Alice B. Toklas (1877–1967) owned a Standard white Poodle bought from a Parisian dog show. They called him Basket, so-named because Toklas felt he ought to carry a basket of flowers in his mouth to complement his stylishness. Stein insisted on bathing him in sulphur water and making him run around to dry himself. After Basket's death, he was replaced by another poodle named Basket II. Stein and Toklas also had two chihuahuas named Byron.

BAT

Beatrix Potter (1866–1943) was drawn to animals and natural history from childhood. Among her earliest illustrations is a pet bat, shared with her brother Bertram.

'Bertram went back to school September 16th,' she wrote in her journal in 1884. 'Leaving me responsibility of a precious bat. It is a charming little creature, quite tame and apparently happy as long as it has sufficient flies and raw meat. I fancy bats are things most people are pleasingly ignorant about. I had no idea they were so active on their legs, they are in fact provided with four legs and two wings as well, and their tail is very useful for trapping flies.'

In fact there were two long-eared bats. One was set free but Beatrix chloroformed and stuffed the other, as she did with several other animals including frogs and a rabbit. She also looked after, and drew, hedgehogs (including one Mrs Tiggy-Winkle), mice (captured in the wild and given the run of the house), snails, a squirrel called Twinkleberry and lizards, as well as a frog called Punch.

Her first pet rabbit as a child was the brown Benjamin Bouncer, an inspiration for the famous Peter. He accompanied the family on holidays and she took him for walks on a lead. Rather spoilt, as well as enjoying treats of buttered toast, he was overfed on sweets which made him ill. On one occasion, he became so befuddled after eating hemp seeds that he was too troublesome for her to sketch. He also had a habit of eating her paints.

Benjamin was followed by Peter Piper. She claimed he was clever enough to ring a small bell, jump through a hoop, and play the tambourine.

BAUDELAIRE

In a letter to his friend Caroline Aupick in March 1852, French poet, critic, translator and cat-owner Charles Baudelaire (1821–1867) complains that his mistress and muse Jeanne Duval had become 'an impediment not merely to my happiness…but also to the improvement of my mental faculties', not least because she was the kind of person 'who drives away one's cat, the sole source of amusement in one's lodgings, and who brings in dogs, because the sight of dogs sickens me'. While it's unclear what happened to his cat, he maintained his stormy on-off relationship with Jeanne until his death.

BEAR

Romantic poet and general ne'er-do-well Lord Byron (1788–1824) spent some of the early 1820s living in Ravenna, Italy. His friend and fellow poet Percy Bysshe Shelley visited him and noted that Byron shared his home with 'ten horses, eight enormous dogs, three monkeys, five cats, an eagle, a crow, and a falcon; and all these, except the horses, walk about the house, which every now and then resounds with their unarbitrated quarrels, as if they were the masters of it'. Shelley then notes that he has also just come face to face on Byron's staircase with five peacocks, two guinea hens, and an Egyptian crane.

However, Byron is probably best known for his pet bear. Informed that he was not allowed to have his bulldog Smut living with him while he was a student at Trinity College, Cambridge, in a fit of pique he bought the bear at a fair in Stourbridge. He installed Bruin in his lodgings and took it for walks – on a chain of course. In 1807 he wrote to his friend Elizabeth Pigot: 'I have got a new friend, the finest in the world, a tame bear. When I brought him here, they asked me what to do with him, and my reply was he should sit for a fellowship.'

After his graduation, Byron took the bear to his ancestral home, Newstead Abbey, where guests were encouraged to play with it.

BENTHAM

As a young boy, philosopher and early animal rights supporter Jeremy Bentham (1748–1832) admitted to throwing a cat out of his grandmother's window to check that it would land on its feet (which it did successfully). As an adult he initially called his own cat Langborne, then upgraded him to The Reverend Sir John Langborne DD (Doctor of Divinity). In his 1843 collected works prepared by his friend and literary executor John Bowring, Bentham admits to feeding Langborne macaroni from his own plate. Bowring describes Langborne as 'frisky' in his early days and a cat who 'enjoyed seducing light and giddy young ladies of his own race', becoming 'sedate and thoughtful' as he grew older.

Here's how Bentham described another of his felines. 'I had a remarkably intellectual cat, who never failed to attend one of us when we went round the garden. He grew quite a tyrant, insisting on being fed, and being noticed. His moral qualities were most despotic – his intellect extraordinary; but he was a universal nuisance.'

BLACK MADONNA

Doris Lessing (1919–2013), author of the story collection *The Black Madonna* (1966), had a cat of the same name some years before the book came out. She also had one called El Magnifico which only had three legs (see also L is for Lessing).

BLITZ

'With love & best wishes to Val & Rita from Dorothy L. Sayers & Blitz Fleming. (P.S. The poem on p.158 is about ME. Blitz).'

Inscription in *Lords of Life: An Anthology of Animal Poetry of the Last Fifty Years,* edited by Derek Gilpin Barnes, illustrated by Kathleen Gardiner and presented by crime writer, poet and advertising copywriter Dorothy L. Sayers in 1946 to radio dramatist Val Gielgud.

BLYTON

Enid Blyton and her siblings were banned from having pets when they were children – except very briefly a kitten called Chippy and some caterpillars in the garden shed – but once grown up the author of the 'Famous Five' series had an enormous number of animals at home including various fish, pigeons, ducks and a tortoise called Thomas. In the 1930s her Fox Terrier Bobs 'wrote' her columns about life at home for *Teacher's World* magazine and his death in 1935 did not prevent his columns continuing until 1945. When Bobs died, she told the gardener not to mark where he was buried in case any inquisitive fans suspected the worst. Blyton says she taught Bob to close doors and wait for the 'click' to make sure they were properly shut.

Her book *Bimbo and Topsy* (1943) featured her Siamese cat and another Fox Terrier dog. In her autobiography *The Story of My Life* (1952) she mentions how while Topsy is very jolly, he also managed to get into the neighbour's garden and kill

19 hens and chickens so had to be sent away. Bimbo the cat, however, she said was far cleverer.

She also wrote about her other Fox Terrier Sandy (who lived in a specially built kennel with Bobs which had two doors and a partition to create two rooms) and Laddie, who becomes Loony the black Cocker Spaniel in her six 'Barney Mysteries', because she says he was so silly, running around the house and up and down the stairs at high speed. Kiki in the 'Adventures' series was inspired by her aunt's pet parrot.

BOND

Michael Bond (1926–2017), creator of Paddington and the adventures of the guinea pig Olga da Polga, had several guinea pigs as pets for many years including half a dozen real-life incarnations of Olga and another called Oksana. He did not cage them, but allowed them to run around the house. He also

had three as a child called Pip, Squeak and Wilfred and a dog called Binkie who once chewed the binding of his favourite childhood copy of *The Swiss Family Robinson*. In an interview for the *Daily Telegraph* he talked about taking Binkie to the library as a child to take out books.

BOOKSHOP DOGS

There are of course 'Bring your pet to work' days, but novelist Ann Patchett has gone one better and lets her dogs roam around the bookstore Parnassus Books which she opened in Nashville, Tennessee in 2011. The first store dog was her

Chihuahua/terrier mix Rose who sadly died two weeks after the shop opened (although Rose's dislike of children may not have helped profits). Rose has been followed by half a dozen others including a short-haired miniature dachshund caled Lexington who happily liked children very much, and rescue dog Sparky – who has earned the title of Assistant Co-Owner and even got married in the shop... The dogs even have their own blog at the shop's website https://parnassusmusing.net

Patchett also argues that her store dogs encourage reading by creating a friendly atmosphere which welcomes readers, along similar lines to the Read2dogs sessions run by the Pets As Therapy charity.

BOUNCE

English poet and satirist Alexander Pope (1688–1744) owned several dogs, all called Bounce. His favourite Bounce was a female Great Dane whom he took for walks as protection when his work *The Dunciad* made him worried about the possibility of threatened attacks from other writers whom he had satirised (Pope was only 4 feet 6 inches tall and among his illnesses was a form of tuberculosis which gave him a hunchback). Indeed, the son of one critic Pope criticised strongly came close to assaulting him and had to be persuaded not to injure him. Bounce must have been a powerful deterrent as no further such episodes recurred.

Bounce relaxed at Pope's feet while he wrote. Pope gave one of the puppies from her first litter to Frederick, the Prince of Wales in 1736 with the collar famously inscribed:

> I am His Highness' Dog at Kew;
> Pray tell me Sir, whose Dog are you?

A later Bounce is said to have saved Pope's life when a new valet attempted to stab the poet as he slept. Bounce, asleep under the bed, apparently heard her master's cry for help and leapt onto the valet, pinning him to the ground until human help arrived.

The last Bounce – a male and not the Great Dane – died in 1744. Pope received a letter in April from his friend Lord Orrery, to whom he had entrusted his dog two years previously, who said Bounce had been bitten by a rabid dog and been put down. Pope's consequent epigram read:

> Ah Bounce! ah gentle Beast! why wouldst thou dye,
> When thou hadst Meat enough and Orrery?

Pope died seven weeks later.

BUDGERIGAR

Angela Carter (1940–1992) allowed her two pet budgerigars, Adelaide and Chubbeleigh, to fly at will around her colourfully decorated sitting room. Her cats Cocker and Ponce meanwhile were kept outside in the garden. In the book *A Card from Angela Carter* by her friend Susannah Clapp, the author describes how the birds enjoyed their liberty 'balefully watched through the windows by the household's salivating cats'. Edmund Gordon's biography of the strongly feminist and magical realist author, *The Invention of Angela Carter* (2016), quotes her as saying that, 'I get on well with cats because some of my ancestors were witches.'

BUKOWSKI

According to poet and short-story writer Charles Bukowski (1920–1994), 'The more cats you have, the longer you live'. He owned a one-eared tomcat named Butch Van Gogh Artaud Bukowski. He said, 'Having a bunch of cats around is good. If you're feeling bad, you just look at the cats, you'll feel better, because they know that everything is, just as it is.' His slim posthumously published book of poems and musings *On Cats* (2015) contains many other considerations of life with felines including how they could be ferocious as well as astonishingly loving.

BURNETT

Frances Hodgson Burnett (1849–1924) showed her cat Dick at the first New York cat show at Madison Square Garden in 1895. Helen Winslow, author of the 1900 classic *Concerning Cats: My Own and Some Others*, estimated Dick's weight at an impressive 22 pounds (10 kilograms), was 3 feet (91 centimetres) long and had a 24-inch (60-centimetre) girth. Burnett also had a cat called Dora.

BUTCH

Butch was a parakeet owned by Marilyn Monroe and playwright Arthur Miller who lived with them in their East 57th Street apartment in New York. When the couple left New York to fly to Los Angeles to film *Let's Make Love* in November 1959, Butch was hidden away but woke up and squawked, 'I'm Marilyn's bird'.

C

IS FOR ...

CALVIN

Harriet Beecher Stowe (1811–1896) called her Maltese stray Calvin after her husband and literary agent, Calvin E. Stowe. Calvin, the dog, could open door handles.

CARROLL

In his book *The Life and Letters of Lewis Carroll* (1898), Stuart Dodgson Collingwood, nephew of Lewis Carroll, author of *Alice's Adventures in Wonderland* and *Through the Looking-Glass*, wrote: 'He made pets of the most odd and unlikely animals, and numbered certain snails and toads among his intimate friends. He tried also to encourage civilised warfare among earthworms, by supplying them with small pieces of pipe, with which they might fight if so disposed.'

CARTLAND

Novelist Barbara Cartland (1901–2000) was particularly fond of dogs, especially her two white Pekingese Mwi-Mwi and Twi-Twi, who starred in her novel *The Prince and the Pekingese* (1979). According to her son Ian McCorquodale, 'My mother often said that "you don't choose your dog, your dog chooses you".'

Cartland also had a black Labrador called Duke who was given to her by the Earl Mountbatten of Burma. At Christmas, her dogs' presents were wrapped and placed by the Christmas tree.

She also had a strongminded blue Persian cat called Flumbo (a ginger cat of the same name also appeared in her novel *Hungry for Love*).

CATARINA/CATTERINA

Edgar Allan Poe's (1809–1849) tortoiseshell cat used to sit on his shoulder while he wrote and inspired his famous story 'The Black Cat'. When his wife Virginia was dying, the cat helped to provide warmth for her in the couple's freezing cottage by lying on her stomach. As a tribute, The Poe Museum in Richmond, Virginia, has two black cats, one called Edgar and the other Pluto, after his famous namesake in Poe's story.

CEMETERY

Some writers had so many pets that they created small pet cemeteries in the gardens of their homes, a practice that became especially popular in Victorian England. Among them was Thomas Hardy (see W for more on his dog Wessex, whose gravestone reads: 'The Famous Dog Wessex/August 1913–27 December 1926/Faithful Unflinching') at his Max Gate home near Dorchester. Many of his cats are buried there, often, like Snowdove, hit by trains on the nearby tracks, although Kitsy sadly met her end strangled by a rabbit snare. Hardy even carved some of the headstones himself.

Edith Wharton (1862–1937) also established a pet cemetery at her home, The Mount, in Lenox, Massachusetts, marking the final resting places of her dogs Mimi (d.1902), Toto (d.1904), Miza (d.1906), and Jules (d.1907). There have been several reported sightings of ghost dogs at The Mount since her death.

There is a small dog cemetery next to the swimming pool at the Museo Ernest Hemingway in Cuba, the last resting place for the novelist's pets Black (his favourite), Negrita, Linda and Neron.

CHANDLER

Thriller writer Raymond Chandler (1888–1959) named his black Persian cat Taki – or rather renamed it as the original spelling was Take but he became exasperated explaining it was the Japanese word for bamboo. He described Taki as his secretary.

In a letter to his friend, the humorist and editor Charles Morton, he explained Taki had been with him since he started writing, whether getting in the way or simply staring out of the window. 'Taki is a completely poised animal,' he wrote, 'and always knows who likes cats, never goes near anybody that doesn't, always walks straight up to anyone, however lately arrived and completely unknown to her, who really does.' He added that he did not dislike dogs, it was just that they required more entertaining.

While Taki did bring animals into the house, including a dove, blue parakeet, large butterfly, and mice, Chandler said she never killed any of them. She also watched gophers.

CHARLEY

John Steinbeck's (1902–1968) Paris-born Standard Poodle Charley (aka Charles le Chien) gained immortality when he accompanied his master on the 1960 US road trip later written up as the travelogue *Travels With Charley*, published two years later. His wife Elaine said she thought it would be a great idea if 10-year-old Charley went with Steinbeck since he could give him a hand if her husband got into trouble. To which Steinbeck replied, 'Elaine, Charley isn't Lassie.' Charley devised various ways to wake Steinbeck when the author was sleeping including rattling his collar, sneezing, and simply staring into his master's closed eyes. Charley also demonstrated his courage by barking at bears at the side of the road when the couple visited Yellowstone National Park, and later his respect for the giant Redwood trees in California by not urinating on them.

CHRISTIE

Agatha Christie (1890–1976) liked terriers and dedicated her 1937 novel *Dumb Witness* to her favourite dog Peter (about which the *Guardian* newspaper's literary critic Ernest Punshon commented that, 'in this dog-worshipping country is enough of itself to ensure success'). The dedication runs:

> To
> Dear Peter
> Most faithful of friends
> And dearest of companions,
> A dog in a thousand

Peter, under the guise of Bob, plays the eponymous key role in the novel which centres on the suspicious death of a wealthy spinster which is investigated by Poirot.

Christie's first dog was called George Washington and her last was a Manchester Terrier called Bingo who was a biter. There is a pet cemetery at her home, Greenway in Devon.

CHURCHILL'S CATS

Prime Minister and winner of the Nobel Prize in Literature for 1953, Winston Churchill (1874–1965) had numerous pets from the time he was 17 and sold his bicycle to buy a bulldog called Dodo.

There were lots of animals at Chartwell, Churchill's home

from 1924, including black swans, a Canadian goose called 'the flag lieutenant', and two brown poodles (the first called Rufus and then, after he was hit by a car, Rufus II, who died in his sleep in 1962), tropical fish and a blue budgerigar called Toby which Churchill allowed to fly around his study. After swishing a cat called Cat which was ignoring him, Churchill made amends when it ran away by putting up a sign in the window saying that if he came home, all would be forgiven. It did so a few days later and received a cream and salmon supper. There followed numerous other cats at Chartwell including the neutered Tango who slept on Churchill's bed and who Churchill always referred to as female.

Churchill also enjoyed pets at work. He described his black tomcat Nelson as 'the bravest cat I ever knew' for chasing a large dog out of the Admiralty and also claimed he was the perfect hot water bottle. When Churchill became

Prime Minister in 1940 and moved to 10 Downing Street, the feisty Nelson drove off Neville Chamberlain's incumbent cat, nicknamed the Munich Mouser by the Churchills, who was found dead the following month in the Foreign Office. Churchill also adopted a stray black kitten in 1953 which was found on the steps of No. 10 and called it Margate after the seaside town where he had given a speech earlier in the day.

His final favourite was Jock, a ginger tom with white paws, who was given as an 88th birthday present by Sir John Colville, his assistant private secretary during the Second World War. Jock went everywhere with his master including Churchill's last visit to the House of Commons in 1964. When Chartwell was opened to the public by the National Trust in 1966 after Churchill's death, the family's hope was that there would always be a marmalade cat called Jock there. At the time of writing we are up to Jock VI, a rescue kitten.

CIGARETTE
Albert Camus (1913–1960), awarded the Nobel Prize in Literature in 1957, enjoyed smoking his Gauloises so much that he called his cat Cigarette (See also U is for Ulisses).

COCKER SPANIEL
Virginia Woolf (1882–1941) taught her Cocker Spaniel Pinka, given to her by Vita Sackville-West, to put out the matches she used to light her cigarettes, a trick she also taught her subsequent pet dogs, starting with Hans, a boxer (other dogs included Tinker, a Clumber Spaniel, and a mixed breed terrier called Grizzle). Pinka also had a taste for eating skirts and book proofs according to a letter from Woolf to Vita in 1931.

Virginia's biography of Elizabeth Barrett Browning and her family from the point of view of Elizabeth's dog Flush was published in 1933 (see F is for Flush). A photograph of Pinka was used for the first edition's frontispiece and dust jacket.

COCTEAU

'I love cats because I enjoy my home', said poet and screenwriter Jean Cocteau (1889–1963), 'and little by little, they become its visible soul.' Among his many design works was the membership badge for the 'Club des amis des chat' (the

EDWARD LEAR AND THE PUSSYCAT

32

Cat Friends club) of Paris which sponsored international cat shows. He went on to become the club's president. Cocteau's own cats were called Madeline and Karoun.

COOPER

Novelist Jilly Cooper has had a black ex-racing greyhound called Bluebell (named after the bluebell wood behind her house) since 2010 and has not had a holiday since then because she doesn't want to leave her. In an interview with the Blue Cross animal charity she explained that Bluebell likes to eat chicken and liver and beef mixed with melted butter and with pieces of paté on top, plus two Digestive biscuits before she goes to sleep. 'I've always had rescue pets because they need rescuing,' she said. 'I think the bond between a rescue dog and its owner is stronger.' Cooper also has a pet cemetery in her garden (see also C is for cemetery), the final resting place for Barbara ('Our most precious treasure') and Gypsy ('Friend to Everyone'). Bluebell prefers to sleep in Cooper's bed although there are seven dog baskets in the house.

CORGI

Stephen King regularly tweets about his Corgi Molly. For example: 'Molly, aka the Thing of Evil, promises not to tear my throat out if I let her clean out the ice cream carton. Claims vanilla "is good for dogs and causes pure thoughts".'

He also used Twitter to explain the dedication of a free short story called 'Laurie' he released in May 2018. 'Several people have asked me about the dedication at the end of "Laurie", the story I posted. Vixen was my wife's dog. We all loved her, but she was a one-woman Corgi. A sweeter, gentler dog you'd never meet. She died early this spring.'

D

IS FOR ...

DAHL

Roald Dahl (1916–1990) kept two tortoises at his home in Great Missenden and wrote in a letter to a class of schoolchildren that, 'We have had them so long I have forgotten their names.'

Various letters to schoolchildren in 1979 reveal that Dahl's pet goat Alma was something of a trial. He described her as 'lovely and intelligent and as tame as a dog and the colour of raw liver', but also revealed that she frequently escaped from the orchard, ran into the house when someone opened the door and jumped onto the sofa like a dog. She also once got into his writing shed and left droppings on the floor which Dahl admitted he was slow to clear up. Eventually, Alma was given away because she could not be kept in the orchard and ate all his tulips. However, Dahl said that goats were 'intelligent and friendly and a lot better looking than quite a few people I know'.

Dahl's favourite pet was his Jack Russell terrier Chopper who he fed oysters and Smarties, four after lunch and four after dinner (now of course not recommended since it can make dogs very ill). The two also used to go mushrooming in the early mornings. The parrot in *Matilda* was named after him, while Alma featured in *George's Marvellous Medicine*.

Dahl's other pets included Eva, a King Charles Spaniel cross, and a Lhasa Lapsul which he said, 'looks like a furry football and comes from Tibet'. He also had a black Labrador called Jelly, a Cairn terrier called Bambi, and an aviary full of homing budgerigars in his garden aviary.

DERRIDA

Philosopher Jacques Derrida (1930–2004) talks about his pet cat Logos in some depth in his essay 'The Animal That Therefore I Am (More to Follow)'. The key section discusses the moment when Derrida gets out of the shower and notices the cat staring at him. This causes Derrida to consider the boundary between animals and humans, whether animal narcissism exists, and the concept of being uncomfortably naked in front of his cat, as well as the more basic question of 'who am I?'

DICK

Philip K. Dick (1928–1982) had a cat called Magnificat, who appears in his novel *The Transmigration of Timothy Archer* as a boisterous tomcat who dislikes strangers, and another called Pinky. Dick believed Pinky was a reincarnation of his friend and editor Tony Boucher, as he explains in the book based on his journals, *The Exegesis of Philip K Dick* (2011) where he recounts Pinky's mystical death in a room that suddenly filled with pale light. His tombstone in Fort Morgan, Colorado, features the carving of a cat. (See also X is for extended cat joke.)

8 OF CHARLES DICKENS'S FAVOURITE PETS

As well as delighting in pet birds (see also G is for Grip), the Victorian novelist lived alongside many other animals including:

1 Dick, a canary, buried at Gad's Hill Place, Dickens's home in Kent.
2 Linda, a St Bernard.
3 Turk, a Mastiff, who died in a train accident.
4 Timber Doodle, a white Havana Spaniel.
5 Mrs Bouncer, a Pomeranian.
6 Don, a Newfoundland,
7 and Bumble, his son.
8 Sultan, an Irish bloodhound, who became very aggressive and had to be put down.

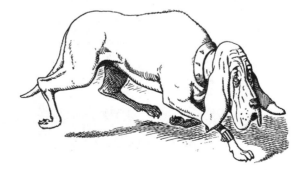

DADDY

When she was a young girl, Sylvia Plath (1932–1963) called her pet cat 'Daddy', also the name of perhaps her most famous poem, written in 1962 and published posthumously.

DICKINSON

Poet Emily Dickinson's (1830–1886) giant brown Newfoundland was called Carlo, a present from her father, who was a comfort to her during her reclusive lifestyle. She wrote in a letter that dogs 'are better than human beings, because they know but do not tell'. In her article 'Emily Dickinson Had a Dog: An Interpretation of the Human-Dog Bond' (2015) for the journal *Anthrozoös*, which looks at the

interactions between people and animals, Maureen Adams argues that Carlo relaxed Dickinson and made her feel protected. 'Carlo's quiet presence helped Dickinson transform inner turmoil into poetry and suggests the transformative potential possible in any interspecies relationship.'

Dickinson wrote very little in the year after Carlo died in 1866 at the age of 17 and said to a neighbour that she believed 'the first to come and greet me when I go to heaven will be this dear, faithful, old friend Carlo'.

DISTRACTION

In his article for *The New Yorker,* 18 August 2018, Norwegian autobiographist Karl Ove Knausgaard raised readers' eyebrows with his – perhaps lighthearted – assertion that his family's pet dog 'undermined his literary project', preventing him from writing literary prose for two years, and posed the question: Has a single good author ever owned a dog? (He discounts Virginia Woolf's as merely lapdogs.) He ends the piece by saying that the first working title of 'My Struggle' was actually 'The Dog'.

DUMAS

Alexandre Dumas (1802–1870), the French author of *The Count of Monte Cristo* and *The Three Musketeers*, owned three cats, Mysouff I, Mysouff II, and Le Docteur. Dumas recounted how Mysouff I would follow him part of the way to his office as he walked to work in the morning, then on his return in the evening he would find Mysouff I in exactly the same corner of the street waiting for him. Mysouff II got into trouble when one of Dumas's three pet monkeys opened the door to the house's aviary and the cat jumped in and ate all the exotic birds inside.

Dumas revealed that his monkeys were named after three people with whom he had argued, 'a celebrated translator, another that of an illustrious novelist, and the third – a lady ape – that of a successful actress' but declined to reveal their names because 'private life must be held sacred'.

Dumas also had a pet vulture called Diogenes and five dogs (consecutively rather than simultaneously), Pritchard, Phanos, Turk, Caro, and Tambo. Pritchard features heavily in the writer's witty book of essays *Adventures with My Pets (Histoire de Mes Bêtes)*, in which Dumas also mentions his other pets including a large blue and red parakeet called Buvat, and a green and yellow one called Papa Leverard, plus a golden pheasant called Lucullus, and a cock called Caesar. He also kept a peacock and a pea-hen.

DR SEUSS

Theodor Seuss Geisel (1904–1991), author of *The Cat in the Hat,* had a pet bulldog named Rex as a child, then as an adult Cluny (an Irish Setter) and Samantha (a Yorkshire Terrier). He kept the toy dog he was given as a boy, and which he named Theophrastus, for the whole of his life.

D IS FOR...

E
IS FOR ...

T.S. ELIOT

Playwright and poet Thomas Stearns Eliot (1888–1965) originally wrote the poems in his collection *Old Possum's Book of Practical Cats* for his godchildren to whom he also recited them. The book later became the basis for the international blockbuster musical *Cats*. Eliot was a great cat lover throughout his life and often gave his cats intriguingly poetic names – as he wrote in the book, 'The naming of cats is a difficult matter'. Here are six of the best:

George Pushdragon
Noilly Prat
Pettipaws
Tantomile
Wiscus
Jellylorum

EPITΛPH

When Lord Byron (see also B is for bear) buried his favourite dog Boatswain after nursing him through rabies, he wrote his 'Epitaph to a Dog', printed below and preceded by the eulogy (the top two stanzas), which was probably written by his friend John Hobhouse. It was affixed to the large marble monument commemorating Boatswain's death at Byron's family estate, Newstead Abbey. A slightly different version was printed in the collection *Imitations and Translations* (1809), a selection of poems put together by Hobhouse.

> Near this Spot
> are deposited the Remains of one
> who possessed Beauty without Vanity,

Strength without Insolence,
Courage without Ferocity,
and all the virtues of Man without his Vices.

This praise, which would be unmeaning Flattery
if inscribed over human Ashes,
is but a just tribute to the Memory of
Boatswain, a Dog
who was born in Newfoundland May 1803
and died at Newstead Nov. 18th, 1808

When some proud Son of Man returns to Earth,
Unknown to Glory, but upheld by Birth,
The sculptor's art exhausts the pomp of woe,
And storied urns record who rests below.
When all is done, upon the Tomb is seen,
Not what he was, but what he should have been.
But the poor Dog, in life the firmest friend,
The first to welcome, foremost to defend,
Whose honest heart is still his Master's own,
Who labours, fights, lives, breathes for him alone,
Unhonoured falls, unnoticed all his worth,
Denied in heaven the Soul he held on earth –
While man, vain insect! hopes to be forgiven,
And claims himself a sole exclusive heaven.

Oh man! thou feeble tenant of an hour,
Debased by slavery, or corrupt by power –
Who knows thee well, must quit thee with disgust,
Degraded mass of animated dust!
Thy love is lust, thy friendship all a cheat,

Thy tongue hypocrisy, thy heart deceit!
By nature vile, ennobled but by name,
Each kindred brute might bid thee blush for
shame.
Ye, who behold perchance this simple urn,
Pass on – it honours none you wish to mourn.
To mark a friend's remains these stones arise;
I never knew but one – and here he lies.

One of Byron's favourite games with Boatswain, a Newfoundland, was to pretend to fall overboard in a boat and see if Boatswain would jump in to rescue him. He always did. When Byron wrote his will three years after Boatswain's death, he stipulated that he should be buried alongside Boatswain. In fact, he was buried at St Mary Magdalene's Church in Hucknall, Nottinghamshire, in a much smaller tomb in 1824.

EVOLUTION

Best known for his works *On the Origin of Species* and *The Descent of Man*, Charles Darwin also had a key practical as well as emotional interest in his pet dogs. In his third important work on evolution *The Expression of the Emotions in Man and Animals*, Darwin describes his black and white retriever Bob's hothouse face – the dejected look Bob gave his master when he thought he was being taken for a walk as Darwin headed out of the house but then realised he was only heading for his plant conservatory rather than for a romp in the garden.

As Emma Townshend writes in her marvellous book *Darwin's Dogs* (2009), he spent a huge amount of time with his canines and they were among the first animals to influence his thinking on evolution. 'He wondered what thoughts they had', she writes, 'he tried to explain their behaviour, he wrote letters to other people on the subject'. After decades of noting his dogs' behaviour – such as struggling to deal with its instinct to chase a hare or respond to its master's call or its capacity for shame over an action – Darwin was strongly of the belief that dogs had a sense of humour, possessed powers of imagination, and had the potential for abstract thought, believing they had 'something very like a conscience'.

Darwin had various dogs as a child (Czar, who was a biter, Shelah and Spark) and as an adult (Bran, Pepper, Butterton, Quiz, Tartar, and Tony, as well as Bob). His last, and favourite, was Polly, a white Fox Terrier who sat with him all day in the dog basket by the fire in his study while he worked. She died a few days after Darwin in April 1882.

F IS FOR ...

FINE

Former Children's Laureate Anne Fine, author of the 'Killer Cat' series (1994 onwards) for children, is not in fact much of a cat person. 'I don't even like cats much, tending to find them horribly snooty and stand-offish', she says. 'I much prefer dogs.' Tuffy, the eponymous killer cat, was based on a cat she bought for her daughter Cordelia as a present but which she said turned out to be 'foul, nasty tempered and ungrateful'. However, she has also recognised that the impressive sales of the 'Killer Cat' books have provided a very welcome income. Fine is a particularly keen owner of Bernese Mountain Dogs.

FLUSH

Elizabeth Barrett Browning (1806–1861) wrote about her Cocker Spaniel Flush in two poems, 'To Flush, My Dog' and 'Flush or Faunus' as well as in letters to friends and family, including her husband Robert, whom a jealous Flush once bit quite badly. The following lines come from the former of these two poems:

> Blessings on thee, dog of mine,
> Pretty collars make thee fine,
> Sugared milk make fat thee!
> Pleasures wag on in thy tail –
> Hands of gentle motion fail
> Nevermore, to pat thee!

Flush gained additional fame when he became the main protagonist in Virginia Woolf's *Flush: A Biography* published in 1933. Though in some ways lighter than her other works, Flush examines the unenviable position of female writers,

EDWARD LEAR AND THE PUSSYCAT

the ups and downs of urban London life, and the interaction between women and animals. The dog is essentially Woolf's mouthpiece and is spectacularly observant of human mores (as well as being able to talk to other dogs) – imagine a canine reboot of *Orlando* meets 'A Room of One's Own'.

In real life, Flush the dog was dognapped three times by a dogstealing organisation called The Fancy, who had the audacity to turn up in person at Browning's door and demand ransom money, which was paid twice. Robert recommended not paying ransom demands, even if it meant Flush might be killed (an unkind sentiment for which he quickly apologised). On the final occasion, Elizabeth and a servant managed to track Flush down in London by locating the wife of the dognapper and appealing to her better nature.

Woolf later described her biography of Flush as a 'silly book' and it was certainly not a critical success, although her friend, the novelist E.M. Forster, called it 'doggie without being silly, and it does give us, from the altitude of the carpet or the sofa-foot, a peep at high poetic personages, and a new angle on their ways'.

FOSS

Artist, illustrator and poet, Edward Lear (1812–1888) often featured his half-tailed tabby Foss (short for Aderphos) in his limericks and sketches. The story goes that the tail was chopped off by a servant to ensure the cat would not stray from home. In his introduction to Lear's book *Nonsense Songs and Stories* (1894), Sir Edward Strachey, Bart, wrote of a visit to the writer's home that: 'At breakfast the morning after I arrived, this much-thought-of, though semitailed, cat jumped in at the window and ate a piece of toast from my hand. This, I found, was considered an event; when visitors stayed at Villa Tennyson, Foss generally hid himself in the back regions; but his recognition of me was a sort of "guinea stamp," which seemed to please Mr. Lear greatly, and assure him of my fitness to receive the constant acts of kindness he was showing me.'

An energetic cat who developed a taste for chewing Lear's letters and provided much-needed companionship in Lear's rather lonely final years, it is likely that Foss was the inspiration for the cat in 'The Owl and the Pussycat'. When Foss died aged around 14 in 1887, three months before his master, Lear buried him in the garden of his villa in San Remo, Italy, and had a headstone erected with the epitaph (see also E is for epitaph):

> *Qui sotto sta seppolito il mio buon*
> *Gatto Foss. Era 30 anni in casa mia*
> *e mori il 26 November 1887 – in eta*
> *31 anni*

> (Under here is buried my good
> Cat Foss. He was 30 years in my house
> and died on the 26th November 1887 –
> at age 31 years)

Foss's age at death was certainly inflated by Lear somewhat!

FREEDOM

Novelist Alexander McCall Smith, author of 'The No. 1 Ladies' Detective Agency' series (1998 onwards), has a cat named Augustus Basil, also known as Gussy, a Tonkinese

(Burmese-Siamese cross). Writing in the *i* newspaper in 2018, he argued against restrictions on the keeping of domestic cats in general which have emerged in Australia and New Zealand as a result of the high number of birds they kill. 'The argument,' he said, 'when it reaches these shores, is likely to be an intense one, but the cat lovers – amongst whom I count myself – will probably win.'

FREUD

'Time spent with cats is never wasted.'

Attributed to psychoanalyst and author of *The Interpretation of Dreams*, Sigmund Freud, but also to Colette, as well as to poet and novelist May Sarton. However, Freud (see T is for therapy) definitely did pronounce to his friend Arnold Zweig in a letter that, 'I, as is well known, do not like cats.'

FRODO

Pulitzer Prize-winning poet and author of *All the King's Men*, Robert Penn Warren (1905–1989) had a Cocker Spaniel called Frodo (see L is for literary names). Warren wrote about him in his poem 'English Cocker, old and blind' which includes the lines:

> ...But if your hand
> Merely touches his head, old faith comes flooding
> back...

G

IS FOR ...

GAIMAN

Among the cats who have lived with novelist, screenwriter, and comic book creator Neil Gaiman are Princess and Zoe, sadly both no longer alive. Gaiman regularly blogs about his pets and described Zoe as a 'sweet, gentle cat who was nothing but a ball of utter love'. However, Princess 'is not amiable, and is only easygoing in the sense that the mad old lady who lives down the road and glares at you when you walk past her house is easygoing if you don't disturb her'. She was a stray welcomed into the house after Gaiman had noticed her living wild, but describes her as feisty, grumpy and happy to indicate petting was at an end by biting the hand that stroked her. As Princess grew older, Gaiman wrote: 'I'm going to have a much harder time one day, months or even years from now, explaining why I miss the meanest, grumpiest and most dangerous cat I've ever encountered.'

Various of Gaiman's pet cats are buried near the gazebo garden office at his home where he works.

GAUTIER

Poet, playwright, travel writer, novelist, short-story writer and journalist Théophile Gautier (1811–1872) admitted right at the start of the introduction to his book *Ménagerie Intime* about his household pets that, while the caricature of him sitting around at home on cushions in Turkish costume with cats wandering all over him was slightly exaggerated, it was essentially true.

EDWARD LEAR AND THE PUSSYCAT

56

Among his pet cats were:

Childebrand – a black and tan favourite, who Gautier said came in useful when he was looking for a rhyme for Rembrandt in a poem he was writing.

Madame Théophile – who was initially dumbfounded by Gautier's green parrot, then geared herself up to pounce only for the parrot to suddenly enquire, 'Have you breakfasted, Jacquot?' at which point the cat ran off and hid under his bed.

Don Pierrot de Navarre – a white Angora who liked to pinch Gautier's pen.

Séraphita

Eponine – part of Séraphita's litter, a name popularised by the eponymous character in Victor Hugo's *Les Misérables* (see P is for poodle owners).

Gavroche

Enjolras

Cléopatre

Later in the book Gautier writes, 'Once a cat has given its love, what absolute confidence, what fidelity of affection! It will make itself the companion of your hours of work, of loneliness, or of sadness.'

A cat sculpture forms part of Gautier's headstone at his grave in Paris's Montmartre Cemetery. (See also S is for statue.)

GERAS

Adèle Geras had a white tabby called Mimi, known as Meems, who she describes as having 'an air of femininity and sweetness'. Geras and her husband took separate holidays for 14 years to ensure Meems was not alone for the night. Previous cats included Pobble (also a tabby) and Toey (ginger and white), both of whom died on nearby roads and were buried in the family garden with their graves marked by rose bushes. Geras has written a short book for children called *Toey* (1994), a ginger kitten, in which Pobble appears, and several poems about Meems.

GIRAFFE

Gaius Julius Caesar (100–44 BC), author of the schoolchild's favourite *The Gallic Wars* as well as countless lost poems, brought back various exotic animals from Alexandria in 46 BC, including what became something of a pet giraffe (or what Pliny described as a 'wild sheep' and other commentators described as a cameleopard). The giraffe, the first in Europe, was exhibited at games in the arena and there is a suspicion that it may have met its end there too.

GODDEN

Novelist Rumer Godden (1907–1998) bought her first Pekingese puppy as a 16th birthday present to herself instead of the Persian kitten her mother suggested, and over the rest of her life owned 35 in total. Dark, with a cream nose and paws according to her biographer Anne Chisholm, Godden called him Piers. 'He became my shadow,' she wrote. Godden's first book, *Chinese Puzzle* (1936) was told from the point of view of a Pekingese called Ting Ling, a reincarnation of a man called Wong-Li who lived a thousand years ago. She later bought a Pekingese called Chini who fitted the description of Ting Ling exactly (cream, with a black face).

GOREY

Writer and illustrator Edward Gorey (1925–2000) – who memorably illustrated T.S. Eliot's *Old Possum's Book of Practical Cats* (see E is for six cats owned by poet T.S. Eliot) – usually owned half a dozen cats at a time, but no more than that since he argued 'seven cats is too many cats'. He always left his studio door open while he worked so that the cats could come and go whenever they wanted, and also allowed them to sit on his desk as he drew. Gorey often named his cats after characters in classic Japanese literature and in his will left his estate to a charitable trust for animals including cats and dogs, but also bats and insects. Talking about his home, he said, 'Most of the furniture has been destroyed by the cats.'

GRIMALKIN

Grimalkin – an archaic name for a cat used in many literary treasures from *Macbeth* to *The Midnight Folk* by John Masefield – was also the name of Christina Rossetti's (1830–1894) cat. Here is her poem, 'On The Death Of A Cat', in which Grimalkin takes centre stage.

> Who shall tell the lady's grief
> When her Cat was past relief?
> Who shall number the hot tears
> Shed o'er her, beloved for years?
> Who shall say the dark dismay
> Which her dying caused that day?
>
> Come, ye Muses, one and all,
> Come obedient to my call.

Come and mourn, with tuneful breath,
Each one for a separate death;
And while you in numbers sigh,
I will sing her elegy.

Of a noble race she came,
And Grimalkin was her name.
Young and old full many a mouse
Felt the prowess of her house:
Weak and strong full many a rat
Cowered beneath her crushing pat:
And the birds around the place
Shrank from her too close embrace.
But one night, reft of her strength,
She laid down and died at length:
Lay a kitten by her side,
In whose life the mother died.
Spare her line and lineage,
Guard her kitten's tender age,
And that kitten's name as wide
Shall be known as her's that died.

And whoever passes by
The poor grave where Puss doth lie,
Softly, softly let him tread,
Nor disturb her narrow bed.

GRIP

Charles Dickens (1812–1870) not only included many animals
in his books, he welcomed many animals into his home. Even
after death he liked them around him: when his cat Bob died,

G IS FOR...

Dickens had his paw stuffed and mounted on an ivory handle as a letter opener.

His most unusual pet was Grip, a raven (see also R is for raven). Not only was he the author's pet, Dickens wrote him into his novel *Barnaby Rudge* as Barnaby's clever (he was said to be able to pop champagne corks) and talkative companion. Here's what he wrote to his friend, the painter George Cattermole, in January 1841 about his plan: 'Barnaby being an idiot, my notion is to have him always in company with a pet raven, who is immeasurably more knowing than himself. To this end I have been studying my bird, and think I could make a very queer character of him.' Grip's first entrance in the book is indeed memorable, squawking, 'Halloa, halloa, halloa. What's the matter here? Keep up your spirits. Never say die. Bow wow wow. I'm a devil.'

Grip also impressed Edgar Allan Poe. He enjoyed the raven's appearance in *Barnaby Rudge*, though commented that it deserved a larger role and set about rectifying this problem as it seems his own famous poem 'The Raven' in 1845 was inspired by Grip. 'There comes Poe with his raven like Barnaby Rudge,' wrote poet James Russell Lowell in 1848. 'Three-fifths of him genius and two-fifths sheer fudge.'

Not long after Dickens's letter to Cattermole, Grip died, a likely result of licking or eating paint, despite being given some castor oil as medicine – this initially perked him up so much that he was able to bite Dickens' coachman. 'On the clock striking twelve he appeared slightly agitated,' Dickens wrote to a friend, 'but soon recovered, walking twice or thrice along the coach-house, stopped to bark, staggered, exclaimed "Halloa old girl" (his favourite expression) and died. He behaved throughout with a decent fortitude, equanimity, and self-possession, which cannot be too much admired... The children seem rather glad of it. He bit their ankles. But that was play.'

But that was not the end of Grip. Dickens commissioned a taxidermist to stuff the raven and mount him in an impressive case which he hung above his desk until his own death. Grip is now on display in the rare book section at the Free Library in Philadelphia.

Dickens soon replaced him, with another raven called Grip ('mischievous', according to his daughter Mamie) and an eagle which was eventually given to the painter Edwin Landseer as it scared Dickens' children. The third Grip was also a strong personality. Dickens' son Henry recounts that when the family's Mastiff Turk was served his food, Grip would nip across to the bowl first, stare out the dog, and eat. The dog was not brave enough to approach the bowl until Grip had flown off.

Grip is also remembered today at the Tower of London where the latest in a line of Grips took up residence in 2012 in celebration of Dickens' birth (and the Queen's Diamond Jubilee). An earlier Grip was the only raven to survive the bombing of the Second World War.

GUILT

Margaret Atwood admitted that she created her 'Angel Catbird' series to deal with her relationship with cats and bird conservation. She says in the introduction to an omnibus collection of the books that she had become increasingly interested in bird conservation and has felt guilty about the number of birds her cats have killed over the years.

H IS FOR ...

HALIBUT

Marcel Proust (1871–1922) is credited with owning a pet halibut in the Monty Python sketch 'Fish Licence'.

HARES

Poet William Cowper (1731–1800) was given three male pet hares Puss, Tiney, and Bess, by the son of a neighbour in 1774 and he often wrote about them in his verse.

Puss spent most of the day under the leaves of a cucumber vine, sleeping or eating, although in one letter Cowper recounts her escape from the house and a chase through the village involving numerous local residents. She lived to be nearly 12 years old.

Bess 'was a hare of great humour and drollery' who died young, but once chased the poet's cat when it tried to pat him on the cheek.

Tiney, though, was described by Cowper as 'the surliest of his kind' in his 'Epitaph on a Hare' (see also E is for epitaph) written after his death aged 9:

> Though duly from my hand he took
> His pittance ev'ry night,
> He did it with a jealous look,
> And, when he could, would bite.

In a letter by Cowper published by *The Gentleman's Magazine* in June 1784, he talks in some detail about the hares' habits and individual characters. He admits that one of the reasons he was keen to have hares as pets was that, 'I was glad of any thing that would engage my attention without fatiguing it.' He goes on to describe how he made them accommodation within his home: 'I built them houses to sleep in; each had a separate apartment so contrived that their ordure would pass thro' the bottom of it; an earthen pan placed under each received whatsoever fell, which being duly emptied and washed, they were thus kept perfectly sweet and clean. In the daytime they had the range of a hall, and at night retired each to his own bed, never intruding into that of another.'

Cowper also had a dog called Mungo, who gave him courage during a particularly bad thunderstorm, a spaniel named Beau and another called Marquis who got on well with Puss after the other hares had died. He also kept various birds including pigeons, goldfinches and canaries.

The Cowper and Newton Museum at Olney in Buckinghamshire, where Cowper lived for two decades, contains various hare-decorated memorabilia including seal fobs, a snuff box, and a stuffed hare. Cowper is buried in the Chapel of St Thomas of Canterbury, St Nicholas Church, East Dereham in Norfolk. A stained-glass window above his tomb shows him reading to Puss, Bess and Tiney.

HEMINGWAY
'A cat has absolute emotional honesty: human beings, for one reason or another, may hide their feelings, but a cat does not.'
Attributed to Ernest Hemingway
(See also C is for cemetery and P is for polydactyl.)

HERMAN
Illustrator Maurice Sendak (1928–2012) wrote numerous books about animals including *Higglety Pigglety Pop! Or There Must Be More to Life* (1967) about a dog called Jennie who, despite having a comfortable life and a friendly owner, wants

to discover the big wide world. The inspiration for Jennie was Sendak's Sealyham Terrier, also named Jennie, who had recently died.

Sendak also had a German Shepherd called Herman (after Melville – see also L is for literary names – although there is some suggestion it was actually named after Herman Goering) and another called Max.

HIGHSMITH

Patricia Highsmith (1921–1995) had many cats. Ulrich Weber, curator of Highsmith's literary archive and estate in Switzerland where she spent her final years, said that her relationships with humans were often particularly intense and problematic and that 'cats gave her a closeness that she could not bear in the long term from people. She needed cats for her psychological balance.' (See also S is for snails.)

HIMES

Crime novelist Chester Himes (1909–1984) had a Siamese called Griot. Himes said he named him after the magicians in the courts of West African kings. In the collection of letters *Dear Chester, Dear John* (2008), between Himes and fellow novelist John Alfred Williams, he asks Williams to source the only cat food Griot enjoyed since it was unavailable in Alicante, Spain, where he was then living. This mixture of fish and liver was called Tabby Treat and, rather reluctantly, Williams managed to help track it down. 'Our cat has always been very difficult about his food,' wrote Himes. 'Rather than eat anything he doesn't like he will starve himself to death… he ate some fresh fish we found in Amsterdam, but he doesn't care for this soft Spanish liver, and he won't eat any of the fish.'

HINSE

Sir Walter Scott's (1771–1832) cat Hinse made repeated, and foolhardy attacks on Scott's hunting dogs until Nimrod, one of Scott's bloodhounds, killed her. 'Alack-a-day!' wrote Scott in a letter to a friend. 'My poor cat Hinse, my acquaintance, and in some sort my friend of fifteen years, was snapped at even by the paynim [heathen] Nimrod. What could I say to him but what Brantome said to some *ferrailleur* who had been too successful in a duel, "*Ah! mon grand ami, vous avez tué mon autre grand ami.*"'

Washington Irving recounts that Scott once said to him that, 'cats are a mysterious kind of folk. There is more passing in their minds than we are aware of. It comes no doubt from their being so familiar with warlocks and witches.'

HODGE

In Boswell's famous biography of Dr Samuel Johnson (1709–1784) he emphasises how much the lexicographer cared for his black pet cat Hodge. 'I never shall forget the indulgence with which he treated Hodge, his cat: for whom he himself used to go out and buy oysters, lest the servants having that trouble should take a dislike to the poor creature.'

Boswell recounts how, one day when Hodge scrambled onto Johnson's tummy for a rub, he mentioned what a lovely cat he was. To which Johnson replied, 'Why yes, Sir, but I have had cats whom I liked better than this', but concerned that this would upset Hodge then added, 'But he is a very fine cat, a very fine cat indeed.'

When Hodge died, he was celebrated in 'An Elegy on The Death of Dr Johnson's Favourite Cat' (1778) by Johnson's friend Percival Stockdale which included the lines:

Shall not his worth a poem fill,
Who never thought, nor uttered ill;
Who by his manner when caressed
Warmly his gratitude expressed;
And never failed his thanks to purr
Whene'er he stroaked his sable furr?

There is also a bronze statue by sculptor Jon Bickley of Hodge outside Johnson's home at 17 Gough Square, London, sitting on top of his master's dictionary and next to a couple of empty oyster shells. The inscription reads, 'A very fine cat indeed'. (See also S is for statue.)

HOOD

Poet Thomas Hood (1799–1845) owned a cat called Scratchaway, one of the subjects in his poem 'Choosing Their Names', at the end of which is revealed the name of Scratchaway's mother...

Our old cat has kittens three –
what do you think their names should be!

One is tabby with emerald eyes,
and a tail that's long and slender,
and into a temper she quickly flies
if you ever by chance offend her.
I think we shall call her this –
I think we shall call her that –
Now, don't you think that Pepperpot
is a nice name for a cat?

One is black with a frill of white,
and her feet are all white fur,
if you stroke her she carries her tail upright
and quickly begins to purr.
I think we shall call her this –
I think we shall call her that –
Now, don't you think that Sootikin
is a nice name for a cat?

One is tortoiseshell yellow and black,
with plenty of white about him;
if you tease him, at once he sets up his back,
he's a quarrelsome one, ne'er doubt him.

I think we shall call him this –
I think we shall call him that –
Now, don't you think that Scratchaway
is a nice name for a cat?

Our old cat has kittens three
And I fancy these their names will be;
Pepperpot, Sootikin, Scratchaway – there!
Were ever kittens with these to compare?
And we call the old mother –
Now, what do you think?
Tabitha Longclaws Tiddley Wink.

HOWL

Allen Ginsberg (1926–1997) called his cat Howl after his controversial poem of the same name.

HUGO

Playwright Arthur Miller (1915–2005) had a Basset Hound called Hugo. His wife Marilyn Monroe (1926–1962) also liked Hugo but Miller kept him when they divorced. In August 1957, Monroe wrote to Miller's son Bobby, who was at summer camp, that Hugo had been playing with a donkey and received a kick on the nose. She added that Hugo also liked to wander off and visit other people, as a result of which he had randomly brought home a child's toy, a stuffed dog, and a woman's shoe, they were thinking of renaming him Klepto.

HUXLEY

Essayist, screenwriter and novelist Aldous Huxley's (1894–1963) first book was *Limbo* (1920) which comprised several short stories and a play. Limbo was also the name of his cat. In his later collection *Music at Night* (1931), he wrote about how humans and cats are alike in the essay 'Sermons in Cats'. This includes his advice to an aspiring writer which includes this nugget: "'My young friend," I said, "if you want to be a psychological novelist and write about human beings, the best thing you can do is to keep a pair of cats.'"

Huxley goes on to suggest that the writer goes in particular for Siamese since they are not only beautiful to look at but also the closest of all cats to being human (he is insistent on the necessity of a tail, strongly advising against a Manx because it is 'the equivalent of a dumb man'). The next step is to watch them every day, make notes, and learn from their behaviour. Among cats' apparent inspirational activities are their ferocious methods of 'getting married', the way the 'husband' tires of his 'wife', and how they deal with infidelity.

I

IS FOR ...

IRIS

Novelist and philosopher Iris Murdoch (1919–1999) called her cat General Butchkin. She and her husband, the literary critic John Bayley, would play a game which involved Iris telling a friend in confidence that she didn't like cats, but that John did, only for John to tell the same friend exactly the reverse.

ISSA

Issa wasn't actually the lapdog Maltese dog of the Roman epigrammist Martial (*c.* AD 38–104), though he did write a poem about her and her owner his friend Publius, thought to be the Roman governor of Malta at the time. Here's the first stanza:

> *Issa est passere nequior Catulli:*
> *Issa est purior osculo columbae;*
> *Issa est blandior omnibus puellis;*
> *Issa est carior Indicis lapillis;*
> *Issa est deliciae catella Publi.*

Essentially, Issa is naughtier than Catullus's famous sparrow, purer than a dove's kiss, more loving than all girls, more expensive than India's gems, and is Publius's darling.

J
IS FOR ...

JAMES

Novelist Henry James (1843–1916) had a small Dachshund called Tosca, named after the eponymous orphan raised by Benedictine monks and then turned opera singer in Victorien Sardou's melodramatic play rather than Giacomo Puccini's opera. He described her as having a 'beautiful countenance'. After Tosca died, James replaced her with a Dachshund named Max whom he described in a letter to a friend as 'hideously expensive... and undomesticated' with 'a pedigree as long as a Remington ribbon'.

JEKYLL

Pinkieboy, Tittlebat, Toozle, and Octavius were among garden writer Gertrude Jekyll's (1843–1942) many cats, all of which she could identify in the dark simply by the feel of their coats and the manner of their purrs.

In *Home and Garden: Notes and Thoughts, Practical and Critical, of a Worker in Both* (1900), Jekyll talks extensively about her many cats and especially Pinkieboy. In Chapter 21, 'The Home Pussies', she admits that she prefers 'cats of the common short-haired kind' because they are sturdier than long-haired ones and the fur looks more attractive (plus they can look after it themselves). She adds that the short coat also allows people to see their beautiful structure 'and every detail of lithe bound and lively caper'. Her favourite colouring is tabby and white as she says white fronts and paws make cats look well-dressed.

Pinkieboy is an interesting character. Jekyll admits that while he is capable of extraordinary activity, he also likes to pretend that he is a bit slow. She writes about him approaching her in a June diary entry: 'It is a perfect summer day and I sit looking down one of the broad turf rides in the copse and see a dark object slowly approaching. By the solemnity of the stately advance I know it must be Pinkieboy. His movements are more than usually deliberate for he had a rabbit this morning. He brought it, half-eaten, to show me. Tabby was following at a respectable distance, occasionally licking his lips as if asking for a share, but Pinkie only looked round and gave a short growl, which evidently meant, "Better go and catch a rabbit for yourself."'

As a gardener, Jekyll is especially observant about the boundaries to each cat's territory. So Tittlebat is the king of the primrose garden and the yew birch, chestnut and bracken that surrounds it, while Tabby reigns in the nut-walk and pergola as well as taking on the role of warden of two gates.

JEOFFRY

Visionary poet Christopher Smart (1722–1771) had a cat called Jeoffry who is praised as 'surpassing in beauty' in his owner's poem 'Jubilate Agno' ('A Poem from Bedlam'). It starts:

> For I will consider my Cat Jeoffry
> For he is the servant of the Living God duly and
> daily serving him.
> For at the first glance of the glory of God in the
> East he worships in his way.
> For is this done by wreathing his body seven times
> round with elegant quickness.

Jeoffry was Smart's only companion during his confinement in an asylum in 1762–3, where he was sent following a series of public religious outbursts as well as problems paying off his debts and an ongoing dispute with his father-in-law. It must have struck a chord with Benjamin Britten who set the Jeoffry extract as a treble solo in the festival cantata, 'Rejoice in the Lamb, Op. 30' (1943).

JOYCE

James Joyce (1882–1941) was attacked by a dog when he was a toddler and the incident gave him cynophobia, a fear of dogs. He did, however, like cats and a letter to his grandson Stephen was turned into the posthumous very short story for children 'The Cats of Copenhagen', a collection of comical cat illustrations and suggestions that people in Copenhagen are not all what they appear to be. Its publisher Anastasia Herbert told the *Guardian* newspaper in an interview that it was 'an anti-establishment text, critical of fat-cats and some authority figures, and it champions the exercise of common sense, individuality and free will'.

K

IS FOR ...

KAFKA

Like many novelists, Haruki Murakami, author of *The Wind-Up Bird Chronicle* (1994–5) – in which the search for a missing pet cat leads the protagonist Toru Okada into a series of adventures – often includes cats in his work. He named his jazz club in Tokyo Peter Cat after one of his pets and also has a cat called Kafka. 'Cats just disappear sometimes', he says. 'You have to love and appreciate them while they're near you.' In his essay 'On the Death of My Cat', he talks about how his Abyssinian Kirin passed away, and how he cremated her and put the urn of her ashes in his household shrine. Among Kirin's favourite pasttimes were rolling around in plastic wrap and playing with empty cigarette boxes. Among Murakami's other cats were Muse (a Siamese, who wanted to hold his hand whenever she gave birth), Calico, Black, Mackerel, Butch, Sundance, Tobimaru, and Scotty. He has admitted that he finds it annoying to keep coming up with names for cats so often goes for something not hugely imaginative, such as Calico.

KEEPER

Emily Brontë (1818–1848), perhaps somewhat surprisingly, had a rather fierce mastiff mix called Keeper. The author of *Wuthering Heights* was very keen on large dogs and she was the only person who could properly control Keeper whom she apparently trained to roar like a lion in the sitting room. Although this may sound unlikely, according to novelist and biographer Elizabeth Gaskell, Emily was once bitten by a rabid dog and self-medicated by cauterizing the bite with a hot poker which she grabbed from the fire. In Gaskell's biography of Emily's sister Charlotte, she tells what appears to be an apocryphal story in which Emily catches Keeper on her clean bedsheets and hits him so hard with her fists that she nearly blinds him, Keeper bearing no grudge and continuing to adore her nonetheless.

After Emily died – the last thing she did in life was to get out of bed to feed Keeper – Gaskell less controversially recounts how Keeper followed his mistress's coffin into church for the funeral service and afterwards became unconsolably mournful, moaning outside her bedroom door 'and never, so to speak, rejoiced dog fashion after her death'. Keeper's impressively large collars are held by the Brontë Parsonage Museum in Haworth.

Emily's sister Anne, author of *The Tenant of Wildfell Hall*, had a much gentler black and white King Charles Spaniel which she named Flossy. Charlotte noted that when Keeper died three years after Emily, Flossy was very upset.

Emily also kept a pet merlin hawk called Nero (sometimes misnamed as Hero elsewhere), which she had rescued on the moor, in a cage, or perhaps on a chain, at home. It was given away by the time she returned from her trip to Brussels where she was studying French and German in preparation for opening her own school back in England. She painted an evocative watercolour of Nero in 1841 which can also be seen in the Brontë Parsonage Museum.

KEROUAC

Jack Kerouac's (1922–1969) favourite cat was a yellow Persian called Tyke. He recounted in his autobiographical novel *Big Sur* how Tyke's death, the night after Kerouac left on a trip to New York, was for him like the death of a younger brother. In a letter to her son on Sunday, 20 July 1960 telling him of

Tyke's passing the previous Saturday, Mrs Kerouac explained that she had buried the cat under a honeysuckle near the fence and told him that the blackbirds in the garden appeared to understand the ceremony, flying around and singing for an hour.

KIM

Playwright, vegetarian, and animal rights activist George Bernard Shaw had a dog called Kim. In his play *Misalliance* (1910), Shaw wrote, 'I like a bit of a mongrel myself, whether it's a man or a dog; they're the best for every day.' He also had a cat called Pygmalion named after his famous play of the same name.

KING

'It might be that the biggest division in the world isn't men and women but folks who like cats and folks who like dogs.'
'L.T.'s Theory of Pets' (1997) by Stephen King (owner of Clovis the cat as well as dogs – see also C is for Corgi).

KING-SMITH

Dick King-Smith (1922–2011) author of *The Sheep-Pig* – or *Babe* in the US – kept Saddleback and Large White pigs at his farm near Bristol. He had a favourite pet pig called Monty who especially liked people to scratch his head and flanks. In his book *All Pigs are Beautiful*, King-Smith said that although Monty was a Large White he never lived up to his colour as he liked to wallow in a pond in the woods. As an adult, Monty tipped the scales at 600 pounds (272 kilograms). 'When I went out to feed him and his ten wives,' wrote King-Smith, 'he would come galloping through the trees at my call, a really monstrous and frightening sight to anyone who didn't know what a pushover he was.'

King-Smith also had a French Lop rabbit called Frank who he walked around the garden on a lead, and a miniature Wire-Haired Dachshund called Dodo. Dodo and his human companion starred in various television series for children including 'Rub-a-Dub-Tub', 'Pob's Programme', and 'Tumbledown Farm'. King-Smith's first Dachshund was called Anna. Because she ignored everything he said to her, he thought she must be deaf. 'But she wasn't,' he wrote. 'She was just a dachshund.'

KINNEY

Jeff Kinney, author of the 'Wimpy Kid' series, has a Portuguese Water Dog called Thunder and as a child two Miniature Schnauzers.

KITTY

J.D. Salinger had three cats called Kitty 1, Kitty 2, and Kitty 3.

KOONTZ

Thriller writer Dean Koontz took on his Golden Retriever Trixie from the Canine Companions for Independence (CCI). She was initially trained as an assistance dog but after six months with a wheelchair-bound owner, she developed a joint problem and had to be released from service.

Koontz and his wife Gerda quickly became so attached to her that when she died in June 2007, he wrote that the pain of her death was so intense that he could not write at all for a month.

Koontz recounts an odd event exactly three weeks to the minute after Trixie died. While he and Gerda were walking in their garden, a large golden butterfly of a kind they had never seen before flew around their heads several times, swooping to brush their faces. Both believe that it was Trixie returning to greet them.

The author of *Odd Thomas* and *Demon Seed* found consolation partly in writing a memoir about Trixie, *A Big Little Life* (2009), which not only celebrates her life but looks at how animals and humans co-exist and communicate. He also 'produced' the ghostwritten book *Life Is Good by Trixie Koontz* (2004) which spawned several sequels, the profits from the series going to the CCI. 'That dog utterly, totally changed our lives, all for the better,' says Koontz.

L IS FOR ...

LE GUIN

'Maybe because writers don't want to have to stop writing and walk the dog?'

Attributed to fantasy novelist Ursula K. Le Guin (1929–2018) on being asked why so many writers particularly like cats. Among her cats were Lorenzo/Bonzo, Mother Courage, and Pard, who 'wrote' various posts on Le Guin's blog giving a cat's-eye view on life, collected in the e-book *My Life So Far, by Pard* (2016).

LESSING

'If a fish is the movement of water embodied, given shape, then cat is a diagram and pattern of subtle air.'

Doris Lessing (1919–2013), whose book *On Cats* includes various of her feline writings including 'Particularly Cats and Rufus' (from where this quote comes) and 'The Old Age of El Magnifico' (see also B is for Black Madonna). 'He was such a clever cat', she remarked to the *Wall Street Journal* in 2008 about El Magnifico. 'We used to have sessions when we tried to be on each other's level. He knew we were trying. When push came to shove, though, the communication was pretty limited.'

LEWIS

C.S. Lewis (1898–1963), author of the Narnia series and an anti-vivisectionist, disliked his given names (Clive Staples) and as a child insisted on being called Jacksie, after the family's dog. The name Jack stuck for the rest of his life among his friends and family. His other pets as a child included Peter (a

canary), Tommy (a mouse) and Tim (an Irish Terrier who hid when he saw other dogs). As an adult he enjoyed the company, especially on lunchtime walks, of Pat (a dog who ate a large part of Lewis's translation of Plato when left alone for half an hour), and several cats including Tibbie and Biddy Anne. Other dogs included Mr Papworth, Troddles, Bruce (whom Lewis grew to strongly dislike), Susie, and his last dog Ricky, a Boxer.

LION

Herman Hesse's (1877–1962) cat was called Löwe (Lion). In his biography of Hesse, Joseph Mileck says that many of the characteristics of Leo, the protagonist of Hesse's novella *Journey to the East* (*Die Morgenlandfahrt*), were based on Löwe, namely 'naturalness, independence, silent graceful walk, fondness for nocturnal wandering, love of birds and attraction for dogs'.

LITERARY NAMES

As a child, Virginia Woolf and her siblings had a tail-less sheepdog called Gurth, named after the swineherd/squire in Sir Walter Scott's *Ivanhoe* (see also H is for Hinse). Other examples include essayist Anne Fadiman's dog Typo, Maurice

Sendak's Herman (see also H is for Herman), Robert Penn Warren's Frodo (see F is for Frodo), and Dorothy Parker who had a poodle called Cliché (see also P is for Parker).

LOBSTER

The French poet Gérard de Nerval (nom-de-plume for the poet and translator Gérard Labrunie, 1808–1855) liked lobsters and once took his pet lobster Thibault for a – probably quite short – walk in the Palais-Royal gardens in Paris using a blue silk ribbon as a leash.

'Why should a lobster be any more ridiculous than a dog?' he is reported to have said by his friend Théophile Gautier (see G is for Gautier). 'Or a cat, or a gazelle, or a lion, or any other animal that one chooses to take for a walk? I have a liking for lobsters. They are peaceful, serious creatures. They know the secrets of the sea, they don't bark, and they don't gobble up your monadic privacy like dogs do.'

Understandably the authenticity of this story has been queried, but Nerval had a strong surreal streak so...

LONGFELLOW

American poet Henry Wadsworth Longfellow (1807–1882) had a variety of pets in his home including cats, dogs, birds and rabbits, but the darling of the household was the Scottish Terrier, Trap. Longfellow described him in his children's collection *Little Merrythought. An Autobiography with a Portrait:* 'Trap the polite, the elegant, sometimes on account of his deportment called Turneydrop, sometimes Louis the Fourteenth.'

His son Ernest, a painter, recalled in his memoir *Random Memories* (1922) that Trap initially belonged to Longfellow's other son. 'When my brother went to war he left behind his Scotch Terrier called Trap who was then getting old and rheumatic. He attached himself to my father and followed him everywhere and spent most of his time in my father's study sleeping on a closed register [air vent] where just enough heat came through to make him comfortable. My father used often to take a nap in the afternoon in his armchair in front of the fire. As the gods nod so do the poets sometimes snore. When this happened it seemed to disturb the dog in his slumbers and he would get up and paw at my father's knee till he waked him up and then would lay himself down again with a sigh of contentment to continue his own sleep undisturbed. There was something so human about this that my father never resented it.'

Longfellow Snr took Trap to The Dante Club, the regular literary supper meetings which ran alongside his ongoing translation of the *Divine Comedy,* and he recalls in a letter to Ernest in 1865 that Trap pinched a partridge from the dining table. Other letters recount how Trap was stolen several times and found through a dog-dealer in Boston, his coat dyed to disguise him.

Trap was probably buried at Longfellow's home in Cambridge, Massachusetts, which was also previously George Washington's headquarters during the siege of Boston. Other dogs included Willie who died from eating poison and Dash, a present really for the children from their Uncle Alexander. In a letter to him in November 1847, Longfellow informs him that, 'Dash is well. He has only eaten one window-sash since you left.'

LOVE

The bibliography of beat writer William S. Burroughs (1914–1997) includes *The Cat Inside* (as well as *Junkie* and *The Naked Lunch*). *The Cat Inside* (1986) features Burroughs thoughts on his life with his many cats, as well as a history of how mankind and cats have lived together, going back to the ancient Egyptians and how they are the natural enemies of the State. His own cats, whom he regarded as having special psychic powers and described as practical and 'pure' creatures, included Fletch, Porch (because Burroughs found him on his porch and adopted him), Spooner, Ginger, Calico (who got pregnant very frequently), Smoke, the Russian Blue Ruski (Burroughs wrote 'my connection with Ruski is a basic factor in my life' – whenever he travelled away from home, he always insisted on a cat-sitter for him), and Wimpy and Ed, who was apparently quite naughty. His last cat was the white Marigay (aka Butch) whom Burroughs regarded as somehow sacred. Marigay was buried with Burroughs' other cats in the writer's backyard.

Burroughs had a longstanding subscription to *Cat Fancy* magazine (a monthly title in North America all about cats for owners and breeders) and kept a collection of back copies. In the last entry in his diary he wrote: 'What I feel for my cats present and past. Love? What is it? Most natural painkiller what there is. LOVE.'

Burroughs was once asked by poet and fellow beat writer Allen Ginsberg (see H is for Howl) if he wanted to be loved. Burroughs replied that it depended by who, but certainly by his cats.

M

IS FOR ...

MAILER

Combative novelist and journalist Norman Mailer (1923–2007) once got into a fight with two strangers (sailors, in some versions of the story) on the street while he was walking his poodle, Tibo. The altercation took place after they commented on Tibo's sexuality. 'Nobody's going to call my dog a queer,' said a rather bloodied Mailer. His favourite poodles were Zsa Zsa and Tibo who produced more than 30 puppies between them. Tibo's dog identification tags are safely preserved with Mailer's literary archive at the Harry Ransom Humanities Research Center at the University of Texas.

MARX

George Orwell (1903–1950) had a French Poodle called Marx, which he notes in his diaries had a particularly impressive turn of speed when taken rabbit coursing. The dog was a constant companion on his long country walks and he used the name as a way of assessing visitors' characters depending on whether they thought the dog was named after Karl Marx, Groucho Marx or Marks & Spencer. Orwell also had a goat called Muriel among the farm animals at his Wallington home. She is assumed to be the inspiration for the character of the same name in *Animal Farm*.

MARMOSET

Virginia Woolf and her writer-publisher husband Leonard first spotted Mitz the marmoset on a visit to Victor Rothschild's home in Cambridge in 1934. Surprised to see a really small monkey suddenly appearing in a garden, they were delighted when Rothschild offered to gift Mitz to them while he went on holiday with his wife Barbara. The temporary arrangement became a permanent one and Mitz – who had not thrived at the Rothschild home and probably suffered from rickets there – became especially attached to Leonard, frequently sitting on his shoulder.

A year after Mitz came to live with the Woolfs, he became especially useful when the couple decided to take a driving tour of Europe in 1935 which included a stretch through Nazi Germany. Both Virginia and Leonard recount in their diaries the anti-Jewish hostility they observed, but that Mitz deflected it away from themselves because he charmed strangers and policemen alike. As Leonard wrote in his biography, 'it was obvious to the most anti-semitic stormtrooper that no one who had on his shoulder such a "dear little thing" could be a Jew'.

Mitz was not universally loved though. Virginia's nephew and biographer Quentin Bell was not a fan of the species, comparing them facially to Nazi propagandist Joseph Goebbels in his memoir *Bloomsbury Recalled* (1995). Mitz, he recounted, was very much in love with Leonard but otherwise in 'a perpetual state of vicious fury; ugly at all times, it became hideous when it vented its spite at the world'. He adds that it defecated so much on its master's jacket that Woolf had to add waterproofing to his sleeves. Virginia's sister Vanessa Bell also described Mitz as a 'horrid little monkey'.

In the same way that Virginia Woolf wrote a dog biography (see F is for Flush), novelist Sigrid Nunez has done something similar in her book *Mitz: The Marmoset of Bloomsbury* (1998) which features incidents such as Mitz untying T.S. Eliot's shoelaces.

MELVILLE

According to Julian Hawthorne, son of the novelist Nathaniel Hawthorne, Herman Melville (1819–1891), author of *Moby-Dick* and a huge admirer of Hawthorne and his work, had 'a black Newfoundland dog, shaggy like himself, good natured and simple'.

MENAGERIE (SEE ALSO B IS FOR BEAR)

It would be an understatement to say that poet Dante Gabriel Rossetti (1828–1882) liked animals (see also W is for wombat). A list of the animals who lived with him at his Chelsea home in Cheyne Walk, London, included a Brahman zebu bull (brought in through the house, tied to a tree in the garden, then given its marching orders when it escaped and charged at Rossetti), a zebra, various armadillos, wallabies, a Japanese salamander, an Irish Deerhound called Wolf, a chameleon, a raven, a deer, dormice, rabbits, marmots, a racoon which hibernated in a chest of drawers, two laughing jackasses, a Pomeranian puppy called Punch, a barn owl called Jessie, parrots, peacocks, parakeets, and a kangaroo.

This was obviously not much fun for the neighbours including historian and mathematician Thomas Carlyle who found the noise unbearable. It could have been much worse though: Rossetti was keen on getting hold of an African elephant but felt the £400 cost was too steep, and also wanted a lion but was persuaded that it would not thrive in London's climate.

In the actress Ellen Terry's memoir *The Story of My Life* (1907) she recounts how Rossetti brought back to his home a white peacock which immediately hid under his sofa. Rossetti tried and failed several times to flush it out and several days later asked a friend to help. On the friend's closer inspection, it appeared the peacock was dead. Similarly, he provided tiny bamboo chairs for his white dormice while they were hibernating. After winter had passed, he showed them to his friends and tried to wake them up, noting how amazingly quiet and still they were…

MICETTO

French Romantic literary lion François René Chateaubriand (1768–1848) had a greyish-red cat with black stripes called Micetto ('kitten' in Italian) which had previously belonged to Pope Leo XII and was bequeathed by him to Chateaubriand at his death. (The two had become friendly during Chateaubriand's term as French ambassador to the Papal States where the writer's love of cats was well known.) 'I try to soften his exile', said Chateaubriand, 'and help him to forget the Sistine Chapel and the dome of Michelangelo.' Chateaubriand described the cat in a letter to a friend as 'very gentle, just like his master [Pope Leo]'.

MINOU

Novelist, essayist and travel writer George Sand (Amantine-Lucile-Aurore Dupin) (1804–1876) reportedly ate her breakfast from the same bowl as her cat Minou.

MITCHELL

Margaret Mitchell (1900–1949), author of *Gone with the Wind*, had various pets including numerous cats, a collie named Colonel, a horse named Bucephalus, two ducks (called Mr and Mrs Drake), turtles, and two alligators.

MITFORD

Jessica 'Decca' Mitford (1917–1996), whose autobiography *Hons and Rebels* is cited by J.K. Rowling as one of her greatest influences, kept a pet sheep called Miranda as a child (all her siblings had dogs) to whom she used to feed chocolate and, as she recounts in *Hons and Rebels*, sneak into her bed when her nanny wasn't looking. She also developed a habit of calling things she liked 'sheepish', a usage which her friend Evelyn Waugh then borrowed for his novel *Vile Bodies* (Jessica hung a copy of it in Miranda's field as a present). Fifty years later, Jessica wrote in a letter: 'I suppose that by now she must be dead? ... Miranda was the light of my life.' She wrote a poem about her as a child which ended:

> Once I took her for a walk,
> My only complaint is she cannot talk
> Me-ran-der, Me-ran-der,
> Soon to the butcher I must hand her.

MONGOOSE (SEE ALSO Q IS FOR QUININE)

Chilean poet Pablo Neruda (1904–1973) kept a pet mongoose, Kiria, who became his chief companion while he worked as a diplomat in Colombo, in what was then known as Ceylon. In his memoirs, Neruda wrote that Kiria was constantly with him all day and night as he worked, ate and slept. Kiria often snoozed during the day on his shoulder and went with him on long walks. 'No one can imagine the affectionate nature of a mongoose', he wrote in his 1974 memoirs.

Neruda also mentions a story when neighbours were keen for Kiria to see off a venomous Russell's viper – mongooses being famously known for their snake-killing abilities. Kiria was released but on edging forward and realising the snake was about to strike, turned tail and fled to Neruda's bedroom. On a later diplomatic posting to Jakarta (then known as Batavia), Kiria got lost trying to follow Neruda through busy city streets. Despite putting a notice in the local papers which read, 'Lost: mongoose, answers to the name of Kiria', she never returned.

Neruda also had a dog called Kuthaka who is credited with saving Neruda's life when he tripped and fell onto railway tracks and knocked himself unconscious. Kuthaka's barking apparently alerted the approaching train driver to stop. Neruda called all his dogs Kuthaka from then on, an appellation he assumed was a name suggestion by a servant when in fact it was Neruda's mishearing of a Hindi phrase which actually meant, 'Shall I bring some dog food?'.

Another pet was a badger called El Niño who was reluctantly given to a zoo after biting a visitor and then their maid in the neck.

MONKEY

As a child, Tove Jansson's (1914–2001) family had a monkey called Poppolino which was more her father, the sculptor Viktor Jansson's pet. In her *Sculptor's Daughter: A Childhood Memoir* she explains how Poppolino once escaped from his cage and ate a model of the baby Jesus, replaced quickly by Jansson's mother and the incident never mentioned to her father. Jansson also had a black cat called Psipsina (which means cat in Greek).

Science-fiction writer Arthur C. Clarke (1917–2008) also kept a monkey. According to Valerie Ekanayake, married to Clarke's diving business partner, it was a remarkably agile purple-faced langur, known as Monkey Baby and Miss Kong, who stole the neighbours' avocados and liked to ride their Great Dane. In his collection of essays *The View from Serendip* (1967) Clarke writes that Miss Kong 'suffers from the unshakeable conviction, based on the flimsiest of evidence, that I am her next of kin'. He says that she enjoyed clinging to him for hours (and happily for him appeared to be more housetrained than Leonard Woolf's Mitz – see M is for marmoset). Clarke also had two German Shepherd dogs, Sputnik and Rex.

MONSIVÁIS

Mexican essayist and biographer Carlos Monsiváis (1938–2010) had dozens of cats and liked to give them intriguing names such as Catzinger, Miss Antropía, and Miau Tse Tung.

He was a founder of the animal shelter Gatos Olvidados (Forgotten Cats) in Mexico City.

MONTGOMERY

Lucy Maud Montgomery (1874–1942), best known as the author of the 'Anne of Green Gables' series for children, had several cats including a grey tabby called Daffy (named after daffodils which she loved), to whom she would read drafts of her work as she wrote while the cat sat on her lap. ('The only real cat is a grey cat', she wrote in her diary, in which she stuck photos of her various cats.) The short book *Lucy Maud and the Cavendish Cat* (1997) by Lynn Manuel with illustrations by Janet Wilson recreates this experience from Daffy's point of view, using quotes from Montgomery's journals about how they worked together. In a 1907 letter to her writer friend Ephraim Weber, Montgomery described Daffy as enormous and 'everything a cat should be, except that he hasn't one spark of affection in his soul... The only things he loves are his stomach and a certain cushion in a sunny corner.' She also admits he had a habit of hunting and eating squirrels which she found upsetting.

But Montgomery's favourite cat came after Daffy. She described Good Luck, also known as Lucky, as the 'only perfect thing I have seen in this world'. Lucky used to run out to meet her when she returned from trips away from home and she also encouraged him to bring into the house any animals he caught, including a snake and a rabbit which was later found upstairs under a bed.

When Lucky died of liver cancer in 1938, Montgomery devoted dozens of pages to him in her diary, writing that she loved him as a human being rather than a cat and that 'few human beings have given me the happiness he gave me'. A year later, Montgomery noted that she often woke in the night and cried when she reached out for his 'silken flank' and he was not there.

12 OF MICHAEL MORPURGO'S PETS
Swimsy (goldfish)
Prynne (Labrador Retriever cross)
George (cockerel)
Puck (Shetland sheepdog)
Sophie (English Setter)
Katie (Irish Setter)
Bercelet (lurcher)
Snug, Bottom, Mini, Simpson and Leo (cats)

N
IS FOR ...

NABOKOV

Novelist Vladimir Nabokov (1899–1977) had a dachshund called Box II who was the grandson of Anton Chekhov's dog Bromide (see also Q is for Quinine). Box II died in Prague where Nabokov says in his autobiography *Speak, Memory* that in 1930 he looked like 'an émigré dog in a patched and ill-fitting coat'.

NAMING

According to satirist Samuel Butler (1835–1902), best known for his novel *Erewhon*: 'They say the test of [literary power] is whether a man can write an inscription. I say "Can he name a kitten?" And by this test I am condemned, for I cannot.'

Writing to his stepmother in 1926, his final year at boarding school, poet and playwright Louis MacNeice (1907–1963) suggested the following names for some new kittens at home:

Old Foss (see F is for Foss)
Barocco
Rokoko
Rodillardus (François Rabelais' fairy-tale cat)
Chat Botté (the French name for Puss in Boots)
Malinn
Fanfreluche (French for decorative frills)
Cydalise (probably taken from the French ballet *Cydalise et le chèvre-pied* which had premiered in Paris three years earlier)
Poll Troy
Dobbin
Queen Anne
Pactolus (the name of the river in Turkey in which King Midas washed his hands to rid himself of his golden curse)

Parthenon
Laidronette (the heroine of the French fairy tale 'The Green Serpent')
Midas
Oenone (the first wife of Paris of Troy)
Quangle Wangle
Amanda
Passionata
Perhaps

NANA

J.M. Barrie (1860–1937) based Nana the dog in *Peter Pan* on his own pets, more precisely on Luath, a black and white Landseer Newfoundland which he had adopted a year after the death of his St Bernard, Porthos.

Luath was named after the collie dog in the Sir Edwin Landseer's painting of 1822 *The Two Dogs*, which was itself inspired by the dog called Luath in Robert Burns's poem of 1786 'The Twa Dogs: A Tale'. In this poem, Luath was a 'ploughman's collie' and discusses with another dog various flaws in human nature. Burns actually had a dog called Luath himself, a name taken by him from Cuchullin's hunting dog in Ossian's epic Gaelic poem *Fingal*.

Porthos was named after the dog in George Du Maurier's novel *Peter Ibbetson* (1846), rather than the famous musketeer (Du Maurier's son Gerald was the first to play Captain Hook/ Mr Darling). The dog was a wedding present from Barrie to his wife Mary. In the script of the play, Barrie specifies that Nana is a Newfoundland, while in the Disney animated version, Nana becomes a St Bernard. In the first stage production of the play in 1904, the part of Nana was played by actor Arthur Lupino in a dog suit.

Porthos appears in Barrie's novel *The Little White Bird* (1902), which contains the germs of the Peter Pan story. In one chapter, Porthos is compared to a 6-year-old boy called David (who was based on George Llewelyn Davies, one of the inspirations for Peter and the Lost Boys whose family Barrie met while walking Porthos in Kensington Gardens). 'The strong and wicked fear Porthos', he writes, 'but no little creature fears him, not the hedgehogs he conveys from place to place in his mouth, nor the sparrows that steal his straw from under him'. But in the end, Barrie says it is impossible to say whether David or Porthos is the most worthy as they both have fine qualities.

NERO

Diarist and acclaimed letter writer Jane Carlyle (1801–1866) was the wife of historian Thomas Carlyle (see also M is for menagerie). Sadly, they had a rather unhappy married life and it was Jane's Maltese lapdog Nero who was her comfort for a decade until the dog's death in 1860 after being run over by a butcher's cart. In a letter to a friend, Jane wrote that the effect on her husband was that he was 'quite unexpectedly and distractedly torn to pieces'.

Nero slept at the foot of her bed and she took him in a basket with her when she travelled by train. In a letter to her husband in 1852, she wrote, 'Nero c'est moi!'. Her diaries reveal he mostly ate bread and water, sometimes with a spoonful of oxtail soup, but rather enjoyed cake.

Among Nero's adventures were several dog-nappings (see

EDWARD LEAR AND THE PUSSYCAT

also F is for Flush) and in a letter to her friend Jeannie Welsh Jane writes about Nero's attempts to fly by jumping out of their library window. However, his jealous attack on a newly arrived white cat, noted in a letter to Thomas, earned him the punishment of a box on the ears from Jane after which he ran out of the house. Nero was brought back but ignored Jane for several hours afterwards.

Nero was immortalised in the popular painting of their home in Great Cheyne Row in London, *A Chelsea Interior* by Robert Scott Tait. Although Jane was not altogether happy about the length of time it took to be completed or about the finished work (she complained he had portrayed Nero 'as big as a sheep'), she did ask Tait for copies of photos featuring Nero which he took in preparation for the painting as she wanted to mount them in a brooch.

A mention of the painting by a newspaper journalist six years after Nero's death caused Jane some irritation. In a letter she wrote that the writer had made 'an almost unpardonable omission, in failing to point out *the Dog—"thinking"!—* thinking, to most purpose of the three, it strikes me! Could anybody look in that dear little quadruped's face; without seeing that *he* was *"thinking"* all this nonsense of keeping him motionless on a sofa-cushion, to be painted, a great bore! And I'll be hanged if either Mr C or I were *thinking* anything more profound!'

NOTHING

Jean Paul Sartre's (1905–1980) cat was called Rien.

O IS FOR ...

OATES

'I write so much because my cat sits on my lap. She purrs so I don't want to get up. She's so much more calming than my husband.'

Joyce Carol Oates, Boston Book Festival, 2010

OBITUARY

Children's author (*Charlotte's Web, Stuart Little*) and essayist E.B. White (1899–1985) owned more than a dozen dogs during his lifetime, whose canine-related pieces are collected in his marvellous book *E.B. White On Dogs*. Although he was especially keen on dachshunds, at one point he considered buying a 'sensible dog' but in the end plumped for another dachshund. 'Being the owner of dachshunds, to me a book on dog discipline becomes a volume of inspired humor', he wrote.

In 1951, White was contacted by the Society for the Prevention of Cruelty to Animals who accused him of 'harboring an unlicensed dog' despite the fact that his Dachshund Minnie did wear a metal licence tag. In his witty letter of reply, White denied the allegation and also pointed out that, 'If by "harboring" you mean getting up two or three times every night to pull Minnie's blanket up over her, I am harboring a dog all right.' He also pointed out that asking for Minnie's phone number was unnecessary as she never answered the phone.

When Daisy, a jet black Scottie and the only attendant at White's marriage, was killed by a taxi he wrote a lovely obituary which was published in *The New Yorker* in March 1932, and also features in *On Dogs*. It includes various of her adventures, including once chasing a horse along a busy street and how she coped in later years with a poorly hind leg. 'She also developed,' he wrote, 'without instruction or encouragement, a curious habit of holding people firmly by the ankle without actually biting them—a habit that gave her an immense personal advantage and won her many enemies.'

White's other dogs included Mac (collie), Fred and August/ Augie (dachshunds), Red, Jones, and Susy (terriers), and Maggie (beagle collie cross). He also had a parakeet called Baby.

O'CONNOR

Novelist and short-story writer Flannery O'Connor (1925– 1964) was keen on birds from an early age. In a short film for British Pathé news in 1932, a young Flannery takes centre stage as the only girl in the world who has taught her chickens to walk backwards.

She started to collect chickens from that moment on, especially slightly unusual ones ('I favored those with one green eye and one orange or with over-long necks and crooked combs') and even made clothes for them – her grey bantam Colonel Eggbert was decked out in a white piqué coat with a lace collar and buttons at the back.

Then she moved on to pheasants, quail, turkeys, geese, and ducks. She first brought half a dozen peacocks and peahens to her home dairy farm, Andalusia in Baldwin County, Georgia in 1952, after buying them by mail-order for $65. Diagnosed with the lupus which would eventually kill her, she thought they would provide good company and cheer her up. The first half a dozen multiplied quickly, living wild on the large property until O'Connor's death. They ate her mother's flowers, her uncle's figs and roosted all over the property.

O'Connor wrote a charming essay about them in 1961 for

Holiday magazine called 'Living with a Peacock' by which point she had around 40 (by her death that figure was nearer 100). Here is how she described their call:

> Lee-yon lee-yon,
> Mee-yon mee-yon!
> Eee-e-yoy eee-e-yoy!
> Eee-e-yoy eee-e-yoy!

Although she enjoyed their company and sent their discarded tail feathers to friends to decorate their hats, the feeling was not entirely mutual. From the start they treated O'Connor with considerable indifference, except when she brought out their food. 'Every time I go out the door, four or five run into me', she wrote, 'and give me only the faintest recognition'.

OWL
Karen Blixen/Isak Dinesen (1885–1962), author of *Out of Africa*, had a pet owl called Minerva. Sara Wheeler recounts in the biography of Blixen's lover Denys Finch Hatton that Minerva died after swallowing the end of a window-blind cord. Some of Blixen's early fiction was published under the nom de plume of Osceola, the name of her father's pet dog. Among her wedding presents which she took to Africa in 1913 were two Scottish Deerhounds – including Dusk, who was later killed by a zebra – a breed which she described as the most 'noble and gracious kind of dog', which add a 'feudal atmosphere' to life, and which fit in very well to the African scenery. 'They must have lived for many centuries with men to understand and fall in with our life and its conditions the way they do', she wrote in *Out of Africa*.

P

IS FOR ...

10 OF DOROTHY PARKER'S DOGS

1   Amy
2   Bunk (a Boston terrier)
3   Cora (a Bedlington terrier)
4   Daisy (a Scottish terrier)
5   Flic (a Boxer)
6   Fraulein (a dachshund)
7   Jack (a Dalmatian)
8   Misty (a poodle)
9   Robinson (a dachshund)
10 Timothy (a Dandie Dinmont terrier)

PARROT

A pet parrot, Loulou, is at the heart of Gustave Flaubert's (1821–1880) famous short story 'Un Coeur Simple'. To inspire himself while he wrote, Flaubert borrowed a stuffed parrot from the museum in Rouen and placed it on his desktop while he wrote. Trying to track down the muse today is a problem as there are various contenders for the role, a conundrum which provides the key storyline in Julian Barnes' Booker Prize-shortlisted novel, *Flaubert's Parrot* (1984).

PEKINGESE (SEE ALSO G IS FOR GODDEN)

Edith Wharton (1862–1937) was a keen dog owner all her life and kept long-haired Chihuahuas and Papillons, but as she grew older she only owned Pekingese including Tootie, Choumal, and Linky (her favourite – she died only four months after Linky in 1937), which she said helped her deal with various challenges including a difficult marriage and divorce, as well as a nervous breakdown. They lived with her in her final years in France where she had special

coats knitted for them and often wrote in bed with the dogs relaxing around her. Like many other authors, she included her favourite pets in her work: four Pekingese appearing in her short story 'Kerfol'. Here's how she described one of them: 'He was very small and golden brown, with large brown eyes and a ruffled throat: he looked like a large tawny chrysanthemum.'

Writing to a friend on the death of Linky in 1937, Wharton said that she had always been able to understand what her pets were saying. 'I have always been like that about dogs, ever since I was a baby. We really communicated with each other—& no one had such wise things to say as Linky.'

Other fans of the Pekingese included Barbara Cartland (see C for Cartland) and Beatrix Potter. Although she once admitted that she 'despised foreign dogs', Potter's two

Pekingese, Chuleh and Tzusee, changed her mind. 'These are both high spirited and affectionate, and less trouble than terriers.' She let them sleep on her bed at night and also recognised their considerable abilities as footwarmers. (See also B for bat.)

PEREC

The French novelist Georges Perec (1936–1982) named all his cats Duchat, although the first one was also known as Duchat-Labelle, Madame Duchat, and Troump-faille. Perec often included cat-based private jokes to his friends in his work, such as the dreamy female cat Lady Piccolo in *Life, A User's Manual,* which refers to composer Philippe Drogoz's opera *Lady Piccolo et le Violon fantôme.* In his essay 'Species of Spaces' he wrote: 'Any cat-owner will rightly tell you that cats inhabit houses much better than people do. Even in the most dreadfully square spaces, they know how to find favourable corners.'

PIG

'Having had one, I think pigs are over-rated as pets.'
Danielle Steel, owner of several dogs but allergic to cats.

POLYDACTYL

Ernest Hemingway (1899–1961) was given a white polydactyl cat – one with six toes – by a sailor called Stanley Dexter in the 1930s. Today, many of the cats at the Ernest Hemingway Home and Museum in Florida's Key West are descended from that first cat, named Snow White, and have the same attribute.

Even those which do not still carry the polydactyl gene so can pass it on to their kittens.

The novelist and hunter had dozens of cats and often named them after famous people including Stephen Spender (later renamed Spendthrift) and Shakespeare (also renamed to Barbershop and again to Shopsky), partly because he believed cats liked hearing an 's' sound regularly. He also taught another, Friendless, how to drink whisky.

After his cat Willie was very badly injured in a car accident, Hemingway shot him to put him out of his pain. 'Have had to shoot people', he wrote to his friend Gianfranco Ivancich, 'but never anyone I knew and loved for eleven years. Nor anyone that purred with two broken legs'. (See also C is for cemetery.)

9 POODLE OWNERS

1   John Steinbeck (whose famous road trip around America was made with Charley, a 10-year-old Standard Poodle – see C is for Charley)
2   Charles Dickens (see also G for Grip)
3   Thomas Mann
4   Gertrude Stein (see B is for Basket)
5   Neil Simon
6   James Thurber (the owner of Christabel also wrote: 'If poodles, who walk so easily upon their hind legs, ever do learn the little tricks of speech and reason, I should not be surprised if they made a better job of it than Man, who would seem to be surely but not slowly slipping back to all fours.')
7   Arthur Schopenhauer (the dour German philosopher who liked his pets more than people owned a series of poodles all called 'Atma', the Hindu word for the universal

soul. He bequeathed a large amount of money to the last Atma in his will to ensure it would be well cared for after he died. 'Whoever has never kept dogs does not know what it is to love and be loved', he said, although when an Atma was naughty he would tell them: 'You are not a dog, but a human being, a human being!')

8   Winston Churchill (the statesman had two miniature poodles, both called Rufus, who ate in the dining room with the rest of the family who were not allowed to start eating until Rufus had been served)

9   Alexander Pope (see also B is for Bounce)

POTTO

André Gide (1869–1951), Frenchman of letters and winner of the Nobel Prize in Literature 1947, had a pet potto, frequently mis-identified as a sloth, called Dindiki who featured in his two books about his time in the Congo. Gide fed Dindiki an unusual diet of jam and condensed milk, which it has been argued may have contributed to the potto's death. Indeed, Dindiki was nocturnal but Gide tried to change its habits by keeping it awake during the day and caging it at night to prevent its escape. In his book *Travels in the Congo*, he describes Dindiki as more attentive than a cat or dog and that while Gide was out walking, the potto would hang onto his belt or neck, or even ear.

PROBLEM PETS

While pets can be much-loved companions to writers, they can also sometimes be less than helpful. J.K. Rowling's rescue greyhound Sapphire prompted the Harry Potter author to tweet in 2016: 'I'd have finished this book months ago if my dog could only make up her mind which side of the door she'd like to be on. #STAY' (More recently she has had similar issues with her West Highland Terrier, Bronte).

Rather more concerning was John Steinbeck's experience with his Irish Setter, Toby. Left alone one night, Toby ate an early draft of *Of Mice and Men*. He told his editor Elizabeth Otis that Toby had 'made confetti of about half of my book... I was pretty mad but the poor little fellow may have been acting critically'.

Along similar lines, but with dubious authenticity, is the story of Isaac Newton's Pomeranian dog Diamond who is alleged to have knocked a candle onto a bundle of the scientist's notes while Newton was answering a call at the front door and which burned the lot (it was more likely a blown-over candle). The urban legend that Newton also invented the cat flap is intriguing but even less believable.

PUG
'He's kind of like Henry James, very stately and stiff and cranky in a good way.'
Donna Tartt on her pug, Pongo

PULLMAN
Philip Pullman had a lurcher called Daisy – a kind dog whom he says once comforted a friend who was crying by putting her head

on the friend's knee – and two pugs called Hoagy and Nellie. These, he says, were untrainable, although Hoagy became quite fat due to being fed treats surreptitiously by Pullman's neighbours.

PYGMALION

Playwright George Bernard Shaw had a cat called Pygmalion. Writer and campaigner Henry Salt, a friend of Shaw's, writes in an essay in 1929 that, 'He was a great lover of cats; and when he came to see us never failed to ask after "Cosy". Were there more kittens? Then he would add in a contemplative tone: "She is a cat of fearful passions." At his rooms in Fitzroy Square there used often to be a neighbouring cat, or a stray, in his company. Once one who was sitting on his window-sill, on the first floor, jumped or fell into the area below. He said he rushed in horror to look out, but no cat was visible, and he feared the concussion had been so great that the animal had disappeared in fine dust.'

Q

Dachshund 1.

IS FOR ...

QUININE

Publisher and dog breeder Nicolas Leikin gave Anton Chekhov (1860–1904) two Dachshund puppies in the early 1890s. The Russian short-story writer and playwright named the black male Bromine or Bromide and the tan female, who became his slightly indolent and tubby favourite, Quinine. On the day of their arrival at his home in Melikhovo, not far from Moscow, he wrote that, 'The Dachshunds have been running through all the rooms, being affectionate, barking at the servants. They were fed and then they began to feel utterly at home. At night they dug the earth and newly-sown seed from the window boxes and distributed the galoshes from the lobby round all the rooms and in the morning, when I took them for a walk round the garden they horrified the farm dogs who have never seen such monstrosities.'

By the summer of 1893 Chekhov recorded that both dogs – nicknamed Brom and Khina – enjoyed long country walks, were rather quarrelsome with each other, and slept in his room at night.

Chekhov was not a cat lover, but he did have several pet mongooses, including a very inquisitive one called Svoloch ('bastard' in Russian) which poked its nose into people's cups of tea (see also M is for mongoose) and a crane who was especially attached to one of the servants. Chekhov bought Svoloch in India and eventually donated him to the zoo in Moscow, although he did note in a letter that he was impressed with its courage and would always win in a fight with a rattlesnake. There is some debate about whether one of the mongooses was actually a civet.

R

IS FOR ...

RACCOON-STRIPED

Journalist and editor George Plimpton's (1927–2003) plump cat was called Mr Puss and was raccoon-striped. His daughter Taylor wrote in *The New Yorker* that 'my father enjoyed nothing more than holding the beast high in the air and making strange, affectionate sounds in that distinguished voice'.

RAVEN (SEE ALSO G IS FOR GRIP)

Truman Capote (1924–1984) had a raven called Lola whom he wrote about in a 1965 essay which detailed all the things she had hidden behind his edition of *The Complete Jane Austen* in his bookcase. This included some false teeth, car keys, money (in notes and change), letters, cuff links, a rose, a button, rubber bands, and lots of string, as well as the first page of a short story he had started and then stopped because he had lost the first page.

REALITY

Schrödinger's is not the only famous philosophical cat. French thinker and essayist Michel de Montaigne (1533–1592) proposed that the qualities of sentience and intelligence were noticeable in animals at a time when they were regarded essentially as machines. He posed this question: 'When I play with my cat who knows whether she is not amusing herself with me more than I with her?' He noted the same issues about his dog dreaming, wondering if it was enjoying the same kind of delights as a human does when asleep (in the dog's case, summoning up a rabbit to chase).

REMARQUE

When Erich Maria Remarque's (1898–1970) book *All Quiet on the Western Front* and its film version made him a target of the Nazis, he fled Germany at the end of January 1933 as Hitler was coming to power, and drove to Switzerland with no clothes or possessions, just his Irish Terrier Billy.

RICE

Interview with a Vampire (1976) author Anne Rice has a cat called Prince Oberon, one called Sugarplum, and another called Mirabel who is the subject of a work in progress about a cat which develops human-like consciousness...

ROLLO

As a child Jack London (1876–1916) had a piebald dog called Rollo ('Rollo and I did a lot of rough romping') and their time together indicated to the author of *Call of the Wild* and *White Fang* that dogs were certainly capable of emotions and able to reason. He wrote about this in an essay called 'The Other Animals' (1908). It was written in response to the criticism of him by President Roosevelt that he overly anthropomorphised animals and was what he called a 'nature-faker'. In particular, London describes an experiment he did when he managed to fool Rollo that a friend of London's had arrived at the house. After fooling him a few times, Rollo caught on to the gag. 'He established a relation between various things, and the act of establishing relations between things is an act of reason – of rudimentary reason, granted, but none the less of reason.' In the same essay, he wrote about how another of his dogs, Glen, showed that he was able to make a choice between two treats he enjoyed, breakfast or a ride in the car. Other dogs of his were called Possum and Peggy (both terriers) and Brown Wolf (Alaskan husky).

ROY

Sir Arthur Conan Doyle (1859–1930), author of *The Hound of the Baskervilles*, had a collie called Roy. In April 1913, he was called to the Mark Cross Police Court in Tunbridge Wells where Roy was accused of worrying and killing a sheep. According to the report of the case in the *Manchester Courier* (and other UK newspapers, not to mention the *New York Times*), Sir Arthur himself cross-examined the complainant, a farmer named Arthur Hale. He pointed out various weaknesses to the case – including Roy's many similar looking sons and daughters in the village, and the farm boy's inability to correctly recognise a dog running at speed – before delivering his masterstroke. As confirmed by the local vet, Roy had weak jawbones and was only able to eat soft food. Killing a sheep was therefore impossible. At this point, the Chairman of the court Mr H.E. Sheppard dismissed the case on the grounds of mistaken identity.

RUMOURS

William Faulkner (1897–1962) owned a series of feist hunting dogs, one of which, called Pete, was killed in a hit-and-run accident. Faulkner wrote a lovely article about Pete in the *Oxford Eagle* of August 1946, focusing on the dog's zest for life. Faulkner is buried alongside his wife, stepson and a mysterious fourth individual named 'E.T.' whose inscription reads, 'An Old Family Friend Who Came Home to Rest With Us', and who some say is Pete...

Jorge Luis Borges (1899–1986) had a white cat called Beppo named after the protagonist of Lord Byron's poem 'Beppo: A Venetian Story'. The story goes that Beppo is buried in the Plaza San Martin park in Buenos Aires, which was a favourite spot of the author's and was viewable from his balcony. His widow has poured some gentle scorn on the idea though...

Thomas Hardy's ashes are buried in Poets' Corner in Westminster Abbey, even though he wanted to be buried in Stinford near Dorchester. In order to comply with the novelist's wishes, it was decided that before cremation his heart would be removed and interred separately. However, Cobby, Hardy's Blue Persian cat, disappeared suddenly just after Hardy died and there is some suspicion that the doctor operating on the corpse left the heart unattended for a while in a dish and found it gone on his return, so the cat was killed and was buried in Hardy's grave to fulfil the spirit of Hardy's wishes...

When Edward Lear moved house he supposedly told the architect of his new home to design it to exactly the same plan so that his cat Foss (see F is for Foss) would not be unhappy...

S IS FOR ...

SCOTT

Sir Walter Scott (1771–1832) was particularly fond of his Deerhound Maida – named after an 1806 battle between British and French forces – and his cat Hinse of Hinsefeldt. In his 1932 biography of Scott, the novelist and politician John Buchan describes how, 'Maida, given him by Glengarry, kept him company on the hearth-rug, and when he was absent on leave Hinse of Hinsefeldt descended from the top of the library ladder and mounted guard on a footstool. Scott used to talk to the animals while he worked, and would leave off every now and then to pat Maida's head.'

Buchan mentions how Scott would often talk to his dogs (Scott also had numerous greyhounds, setters and terriers including Camp, Nimrod, Spice, Triton and Ginger) as he worked, speaking to them as friends rather than their owner. He buried Camp close to the window where he usually wrote.

But it was Maida (1816–1824) who was his favourite and she features prominently in the white Carrara marble statue (see also S is for statue) next to the novelist in the Scott Monument by Sir John Steell in Princes Street Gardens, Edinburgh. There is another statue of Maida by the front door at Scott's home Abbotsford near Melrose with an inscription which reads:

> *Maidae marmorea dormis sub imagine Maida*
> *Ante fores domini sit tibi terra levis*

which Walter Scott translated as:

> Beneath the sculptured form which late you wore
> Sleep soundly, Maida, at your master's door

SIAMESE

Patricia Highsmith (see also H is for Highsmith and S is for snails) made a huge number of sketches of cats and was particularly fond of one called Ripley and another called Spider, black and partly Siamese, which she gave to writer Muriel Spark in 1968 when she moved from Italy to Suffolk. In her biography *The Talented Miss Highsmith* (2009), Joan Schenkar quotes Spark on Spider: 'You could tell he had been a writer's cat. He would sit by me, seriously, as I wrote, while all my other cats filtered away.' Highsmith dedicated her novel *The Glass Cell* (1964) to Spider and talks about the importance of cats to writers in her 1988 novel *A Far Cry from Kensington*:

'For concentration you need a cat... and the tranquillity of the cat will gradually come to affect you, sitting there at your desk, so that all the excitable qualities that impede your concentration compose themselves and give you back the self-command it has lost.'

SIMON

Francesca Simon, author of the 'Horrid Henry' series, had a Tibetan spaniel called Shanti.

She describes her as a headstrong but calm dog who was scared of other dogs but quite happily dealt with the noise of fireworks and was the ideal dog for a writer because she slept and snored under her desk when she was working.

SITWELL

Poet Edith Sitwell (1887–19640 had cats called Shadow (a Siamese), Leo, and Belaker, and as a child a pet peacock called Peaky with whom she often used to go for walks in the gardens of the family home Renishaw Hall in Derbyshire with her arm around Peaky's neck. In her autobiography *Taken Care Of*, Sitwell recounts how Peaky would wait outside her mother's bedroom windows every day at 9 a.m. for Edith to come and say good morning, shrieking in reply. After several months of their walks, Edith's father bought a peahen as a companion for Peaky who thereupon jilted Edith entirely. Sitwell also notes that at the same time she had a puffin with a wooden leg and a baby owl who used to sleep on her shoulder.

SMITH

Dodie Smith (1896–1990), author of *The Hundred and One Dalmatians*, had half a dozen Dalmatians, including one called Pongo who was given to her in 1934 as a present. After living in America for several years, Smith and her husband were keen to return home to England but delayed the move because they wanted to avoid putting their dogs into quarantine. Her final Dalmatian was Charley who was a much-appreciated companion in her later years after the death of her husband Alec, even though Charley was so boisterous he often knocked her over when he jumped up to welcome her into a room. She provided £2,000 for 'the utmost care and protection of Charley' in her will but he died less than a month after her in 1990.

SNAILS

Patricia Highsmith (see also S is for Siamese) kept around 300 snails as pets at her home in Suffolk and took a selection of them with her when she travelled, including abroad, often hidden in boxes or about her person. She also took them to dinner parties in her handbag, in which she also kept lettuce for them to feed on. When she decided to stop keeping them as pets, she simply let them all out into the garden and many naturally moved next door to her neighbour's.

SOUTHEY

Poet Laureate Robert Southey (1774–1843) liked to give his cats impressive names including:

The Most Noble the Archduke Rumpelstiltzchen, Marquis Macbum, Earl Tomlemagne, Baron Raticide, Waowhler, and Skaratch (known as Rumpel and buried in Southey's orchard)
Lord Nelson (later Baron, Viscount and Earl, for services to catching rats)

Sir Thomas Dido
Madame Catalani
Bona Marietta
Othello
Virgil
Hurlyburlypuss
Pulcheria
Madame Bianchi
Prester John (later renamed Pope Joan)
Zombi
William Rufus
Danayn le Roux

As his son Charles observed: 'He rejoiced in bestowing upon them the strangest appellations; and it was not a little amusing to see a kitten answer to the name of some Italian singer or Indian chief, or hero of a German fairy tale, and often names and titles were heaped one upon another, till the possessor, unconscious of the honour conveyed, used to "set up his eyes and look" in wonderment.'

In 1826, while he was on a trip to Holland, Southey wrote to his young son Cuthbert: 'I hope Rumpelstiltzchen has recovered his health, and that Miss Cat is well; and I should like to know whether Miss Fitzrumpel has been given away, and if there is another kitten. The Dutch cats do not speak exactly the same language as the English ones. I will tell you how they talk when I come home.'

STARLING

A prolific letter-writer as well as composer, Wolfgang Amadeus Mozart (1756–1791) had a pet starling which, so

S IS FOR...

the story goes, the great man bought in May 1784. This was not an impulse buy. As he walked past the shop, the bird started whistling the theme from Mozart's Piano Concerto No. 17 in G Major, which Mozart had finished the month before (although there were some alterations – apparently the bird kept singing G sharp instead of G natural). This was all the more strange, since the first public performance recorded was in June...

One explanation is that Mozart had visited the shop before and liked to hum and whistle, so the starling, a breed noted for its mimic abilities, could have picked it up then. The bird lived with the composer for three years until its death, the same week as Mozart's father. The starling was buried in Mozart's garden after a long funeral procession of the composer's friends. At the graveside he recited a poem about it which he had written himself which starts:

> Hier ruht ein lieber Narr,
> Ein Vogel Staar.
> Noch in den besten Jahren
> Musst er erfahren
> Des Todes bittern Schmerz

which celebrates his starling as a bit of a barmy bird who died in the prime of life. Those interested in a much fuller account of the relationship should read the excellent *Mozart's Starling* (2017) by Lyanda Lynn Haupt.

Mozart also had a childhood canary and another towards the end of his life.

STATUE

Crime writer and playwright Dorothy L. Sayers (1893–1957) is immortalised with her cat Blitz at her feet in a statue in her hometown of Witham, Essex. She also had a cat called Timothy for whom she wrote a poem on his passing which ends:

> When the Ark of the new life grounds upon Ararat
> Grant us to carry into the rainbow's light,
> In a basket of gratitude, the small, milk-white
> Silken identity of Timothy, our cat.

There is also a bronze statue of the Finnish poet Edith Södergran (1892–1923) with her cat Totti in Roschino, Russia, where they spent several summers. (See also H is for Hodge and U is for Ulisses.)

T

IS FOR ...

TALKING

Known today particularly for his science fiction, H.G .Wells (1886–1946) had a cat called Mr Peter Wells who pointedly left any room in which somebody talked too long or at too high a volume. In his novel *The World of William Clissold* Wells wrote, 'The cat, which is a solitary beast, is single minded and goes its way alone, but the dog, like his master, is confused in his mind.'

TARTT

Donna Tartt, author of *The Secret History* (1992), has a pug called Pongo. She once said that while they both have friends of their own species, their favourite company is each other's.

THAÏKE

Hergé, the creator of Tintin and his dog Snowy, was actually fonder of cats than dogs. Thaïke was his Siamese and a very similar one appeared for the first time in *The Seven Crystal Balls*, going on to appear in four further books. Hergé, real name Georges Remi (1907–1983), gave his model of the fictional Sir Francis Haddock's ship the *Unicorn*, which plays a key part in his books *The Secret of the Unicorn* and *Red Rackham's Treasure*, to his vet in 1960 to reward him for taking such good care of his cats.

THERAPY

Sigmund Freud (1856–1939), author of *The Ego and the Id*, had a number of Chow Chow dogs, including one called Yofi/ Jofi ('beauty' in Hebrew), who often sat in on his sessions with patients as Freud believed she would help patients relax, while at the same time help him to assess the patient's state of mind because they were more relaxed and spoke more frankly when Jofi was in the room rather than feeling immediately judged. Psychiatrist Roy Grinker recounts how he was treated by Freud and Jofi in a session in 1932 – if Jofi went to the door and scratched to be let out, Freud would comment that this indicated Jofi did not approve of what Grinker was saying. But when she jumped on Grinker's lap, Freud suggested Jofi was excited that Grinker had discovered the source of his anxiety.

She also appears to have been a good timekeeper and indicated that the session was over by yawning and wandering around. Dogs, wrote Freud, provide 'affection without ambivalence'. His interest in them was set off when his daughter Anna introduced him to her lively German Shepherd, Wolf.

In a letter to Russian-born psychoanalyst Lou Andreas-Salomé, Freud wrote, 'I miss her now almost as much as my cigar. She is a charming creature, so interesting in her feminine characteristics, too, wild, impulsive, intelligent and yet not so dependent as dogs often are.' He is also reputed to have said, 'Dogs love their friends and bite their enemies, quite unlike people.' (See also F is for Freud.)

THOMPSON

Hunter S. Thompson (1937–2005) created the kind of pet menagerie (see also M is for menagerie) you would expect from an infamous Gonzo journalist. His pets included a Doberman called Agar and another called Bronco, whom he allegedly taught to attack on the command word 'Nixon', as well as a monkey with a drink problem which, rumour has it, committed suicide from his hotel balcony.

Thompson certainly had numerous peacocks at his Owl

Farm compound in Aspen about whom he was very protective. However, his friend and collaborator, the illustrator Ralph Steadman, has also commented in newspaper interviews about Thompson's hatred for his pet myna bird, Edward, which he kept in a cage. According to Steadman, Thompson would suddenly, and for no particular reason, whack the side of the cage and shout at Edward that he was going to kill him and eat him. Thompson also had two Siamese cats, Caesar and Pele.

TIGER

The most successful book by French novelist and critic Jules Husson Fleury (1821–1889) – who wrote under the name Champfleury – was his volume on cats, *Les Chats, histoire, moeurs, observations, anecdotes* (1869). This featured an image of Victor Hugo's cat Chanoine and a handwritten note

by Hugo including a quote by poet and playwright Joseph Méry, 'God made the cat to give man the pleasure of stroking a tiger.' (*'Dieu a fait le chat pour donner l'homme le plaisir de caresser le tigre.'*)

TOLKIEN
'I fear that to me Siamese cats belong to the fauna of Mordor, but you need not tell the cat breeder that.'

J.R.R. Tolkien (1892–1973), in a letter to his publishers Allen & Unwin when they were approached by a cat breeder who wanted to name a litter of kittens after characters in *The Lord of the Rings*.

TORTOISES
Novelist and playwright Lion Feuchtwanger (1884–1958) fled Nazi Germany in 1933, sadly leaving behind his terrarium and pet lizards. He made his new home in California where he kept two tortoises as pets, each one marked with his phone number in case they got lost and needed a helping hand to get back.

TURTLES
'A Song of Ice and Fire' creator George R.R. Martin kept tiny turtles when he was a young boy because the housing project in New Jersey where he lived did not allow cats or dogs as pets. Martin housed his turtles in a toy tin castle and pretended they were kings and knights, gave them names, and made up stories about their adventures – these were the forerunners for what became the escapades in 'A Game of Thrones'. Unfortunately, despite careful feeding, the turtles all

died quite quickly (sometimes after escaping from the castle) which he attributed to their sinister plots for supremacy... His fondness for turtles has not dimmed – he wore a small turtle badge for the 2018 Emmy awards.

TWAIN

'I simply can't resist a cat, particularly a purring one', Mark Twain/Samuel Clemens (1835–1910) wrote in his notebook. 'They are the cleanest, cunningest, and most intelligent things I know, outside of the girl you love, of course.' However, his most famous saying about felines is the very widely quoted, 'When a man loves cats, I am his friend and comrade, without further introduction.'

Twain had many cats at his farm in Connecticut including Bambino whom he found a consolation when his wife Livy died. When Bambino went astray, Twain published a notice in the *New York American* newspaper offering a $5 reward for its safe return: 'Large and intensely black; thick, velvety fur; has a faint fringe of white hair across his chest; not easy to find in ordinary light.' Happily, Bambino was found and reunited with Twain.

Among his other cats were Apollinaris, Zoroaster, Beezelbub, Tammany and Blatherskite, which he said were chosen to help his children practise their pronunciation. He also took to renting cats when he went on holiday in New Hampshire, including Sackcloth and Ashes.

U

IS FOR ...

ULISSES

'Qualquer gato, qualquer cachorro vale mais do que a literatura.'
Brazilian writer Clarice Lispector's belief that any cat, any dog
is worth more than literature

Lispector (1920–1977) had a mongrel called Ulisses and
found him a comfort after her divorce, although he had a
strange habit of eating any half-smoked cigarettes he found in
ashtrays. There is a life-size statue of her with Ulisses sitting
on a wall at Leme Beach, Copacabana, Rio de Janeiro, created
by sculptor Edgar Duvivier in 2016.

UNTRUE

An intriguing and popular story about Virgil (70 BC–19
BC), author of *The Aeneid*, contends that he had a pet fly for
whom he staged an elaborate funeral with mourners and
built a hugely expensive mausoleum, essentially to avoid
a government land grab of his property. Sadly, the story is
almost certainly completely untrue.

V IS FOR ...

VERNE

Novelist Jules Verne (1828–1905) had a dog called Follet.

VONNEGUT

'I cannot distinguish between the love I have for people and the love I have for dogs', wrote Kurt Vonnegut (1922–2007) in *Slapstick or Lonesome No More*. Vonnegut had a Lhasa Apso dog called Pumpkin.

W IS FOR ...

WALKER

In *The World Has Changed: Conversations with Alice Walker* (2010), the author of *The Color Purple* talks about her cat which she says has one broken and one outsized tooth. To some people this might look odd, but to Walker, 'I look at her and see the absolute perfection – the charming perfection – of her imperfection.' In an essay called 'Frida, The Perfect Familiar', Walker wrote about her other cats including Willis (rescued from New York's Willis Avenue Bridge), Tuscaloosa (a comfort to her during her divorce), and Frida (a jumpy long-haired calico named after the artist Frida Kahlo). According to Walker, Frida enjoyed quiet music, liked to go for walks like a dog, and understood commands in English.

WALLACE

David Foster Wallace (1962–2008) had a black Labrador Retriever called Jeeves as well as three others called The Drone (a stray who attached himself to Wallace while out jogging), Werner and Bella. He was particularly fond of rescue dogs who had suffered a hard life or were difficult to handle and even briefly considered giving up writing and opening a dog shelter. In *David Foster Wallace: The Last Interview* he says, 'After a while I got so I actually needed one or more dogs around in order to be comfortable enough to feel like working.'

WATTERSON

Bill Watterson, the creator of Calvin and Hobbes, had a cat called Sprite who is partly the model for Hobbes. 'Sprite not only provided the long body and facial characteristics for Hobbes, she also was the model for his personality', says Watterson. 'She was good-natured, intelligent, friendly, and enthusiastic in a sneaking-up-and-pouncing sort of way. Sprite suggested the idea of Hobbes greeting Calvin at the door in midair at high velocity.'

WESSEX

Thomas Hardy was especially fond of his Fox Terrier Wessex (see also C is for cemetery) even though visitors were more guarded about him. Wessex was allowed to wander around on top of the dining room table during meals and often tried to eat guests' food. He also bit trouser legs, servants, and the postman. On the plus side, he enjoyed listening to the radio. Hardy only wrote about Wessex after the dog's death in 1926 aged 13, including the first stanza of this elegy from the canine's point of view beyond the grave:

> Do you think of me at all,
> Wistful ones?
> Do you think of me at all
> As if nigh?
> Do you think of me at all
> At the creep of evenfall,
> Or when the sky-birds call
> As they fly?

Another from Wessex's perspective was 'A Popular Personage at Home':

> I live here: 'Wessex' is my name:
> I am a dog known rather well:
> I guard the house but how that came
> To be my whim I cannot tell.

With a leap and a heart elate I go
At the end of an hour's expectancy
To take a walk of a mile or so
With the folk I let live here with me.

Hardy also had cats including one named
Kiddleywinkempoops (or Trot for short).

WILDER

Laura Ingalls Wilder (1867–1957), and her husband Almanzo,
had an Airedale Terrier called Nero while she was writing the
'Little House on the Prairie' books. Nero came along with
them on a visit to South Dakota in 1931 and Wilder's travel
diary shows that he disliked the heat and the city traffic, but
did enjoy munching ice cream and hamburgers.

Other dogs included Shep and Inky about whom she asks
for regular updates in her collection of letters *West From Home*
(1974), written to Almanzo while she was in San Francisco in
1915. She also mentioned Shep in her columns about rural
life for the *Missouri Ruralist* magazine, especially about him
trying to sit up and shake hands but losing his balance. She
noticed him practising by himself on the back porch until he
had perfected the technique. Wilder also had a blind French
poodle called Incubus.

WILL

The first American to win the Nobel Prize in Literature,
playwright Eugene O'Neill (1888–1953) was very attached
to his Dalmatian Blemie (1927–1940). Towards the end of
Blemie's life, O'Neill put together a touching last will and
testament as if written by Blemie himself which sets out that,

'There is nothing of value I have to bequeath except my love and my faith', and encourages his Mistress and Master to have another dog after Blemie has gone. It ends: 'One last word of farewell, Dear Master and Mistress. Whenever you visit my grave, say to yourselves with regret but also with happiness in your hearts at the remembrance of my long happy life with you: "Here lies one who loved us and whom we loved." No matter how deep my sleep I shall hear you, and not all the power of death can keep my spirit from wagging a grateful tail.'

Blemie's gravestone at O'Neill's home in California reads, 'Sleep in peace, faithful pet.'

WILLIAM CARLOS WILLIAMS

Poet William Carlos Williams (1883–1963) had a Shetland sheepdog called Stormy and wrote his final poem about him:

> what name could
> better
> explode from
>
> a sleeping pup
> but this
> leaping
>
> to his feet
> Stormy! Stormy!
> Stormy!

WILLIAMS

Playwright Tennessee Williams had a black Persian cat called Sabbath.

WILSON

Children's writer Dame Jacqueline Wilson did not have pets as a child growing up in Surrey because council-house rules did not allow them. Instead she had a Pekingese toy called Vip and began a collection of china animals on her bedroom windowsill. Since then, she has become an ambassador for the Battersea Dogs & Cats Home from where her pets have come – Jacob and Lily (both grey and white cats) and Jackson (a black Patterdale Terrier). 'Friends told me to get a cat,' she told the *New Statesman* magazine, 'because I'd relax and stop worrying if it sat on my lap purring. Well, I have a splendid rescue cat called Jacob but he's such a sensitive soul that I worry about him terribly.'

WOMBAT

Dante Gabriel Rossetti (see M is for menagerie) used to spend hours at the wombat section of the zoo in London's Regent Park until he made his mind up to buy one of his own in 1869 which he called Top. Top was allowed to snooze at the dinner table during meals and had a habit of following people around the house. Rossetti described him as 'a Joy, a Triumph, a Delight, a Madness' and made a sketch of him on a leash held by Jane Morris, his lover and wife of the writer and artist William (whose nickname was Topsy). Both Top and Jane are pictured with halos.

Meanwhile his poet sister, Christina wrote a poem in Italian 'O Uommibatto', in which she described Top as 'agil,

I never reared a young Wombat
To glad me with his pin-hole eye,
But when he most was sweet & fat
And tail-less, he was sure to die!

giocondo' (nimble, cheerful), '*irsuto e tondo*' (hairy and round). Thanks to Top, something of a wombat craze broke in London, especially among the pre-Raphaelites. Rossetti wrote the following verse about him:

> Oh how the family affections combat
> Within this heart, and each hour flings a bomb at

My burning soul! Neither from owl nor from bat
Can peace be gained until I clasp my wombat.

Sadly, Top died suddenly and unexpectedly only a few months after Rossetti bought him; not, as James McNeill Whistler once claimed, due to eating a box of cigars. The poet had Top stuffed and put on display in the entrance hall of his home.

WODEHOUSE

P.G. Wodehouse (1881–1975) loved his dogs so much that he remained in France, where he was living with them and his wife Ethel in 1939, rather than returning to England because of the problematic quarantine laws. As a result, Wodehouse was interned by the invading German army. Wodehouse was particularly fond of Pekingese but was also a generous supporter of organisations that looked after stray dogs in general.

In 1971, he wrote an article for the *New York Times* bemoaning the trend for visitors to Long Island to leave their pets behind at the end of their vacation. 'It is this that has led to what some people might consider a superabundance, if that is the word I want, of dogs and cats in the Wodehouse home', he wrote, noting that there were four dogs and seven cats in his house as he wrote. He added that the cats (including Poonah, who was black and white) and dogs (such as Bill the Foxhound and a Dachshund called Jed) always got on very well and never fought.

WORDSWORTH

Pepper was William Wordsworth's (1770–1850) dog when he lived in Dove Cottage with his sister Dorothy. Pepper was a gift from Sir Walter Scott who named dogs according to their colour.

X IS FOR …

EXTENDED CAT JOKE

Philip K. Dick includes an extended cat joke in his novel *The Three Stigmata of Palmer Eldritch* (1965) which concentrates on religious beliefs. A cat eats a five pound T-bone steak intended for a dinner party. The guests suggest weighing the cat to check, and it comes up at exactly five pounds. Now they think they know what happened until somebody asks, 'But where's the cat?'

Y

IS FOR ...

YORKSHIRE

L. Frank Baum (1856–1919) was kind to animals and he and his wife Maud had dogs in their home, although she was the one who mostly looked after them. His most famous animal creation is Toto in his children's adventure *The Wonderful Wizard of Oz*. Toto is not definitively named as a Yorkie but Baum describes him as 'a little black dog with long silky hair and small black eyes that twinkled merrily on either side of his funny, wee nose', and he was illustrated in the first edition by artist W.W. Denslow as a Yorkshire Terrier (although in the film Toto was played by a Cairn Terrier).

Amy Tan has had several Yorkshire terriers called King Bombo, Bubba Zo, Lilliput and Frankie, whose full name was Champion Tiptop Come Fly With Me. As well as sitting on her lap while she works ('they adore me no matter how many bad sentences I write', she explains in the biography *Amy Tan: Author Extraordinaire* (2009) by Tamra Orr), she regularly takes them on book tours to make the travelling less lonely.

Z

IS FOR ...

4 CATS BEGINNING WITH Z OWNED BY THÉOPHILE GAUTIER (see also G for Gautier).

Zuleika

Zulema

Zobeide

Zizi

ZADIG

Novelist and scriptwriter Elinor Glyn (1864–1943) had a cat called Zadig and another named Candide, a tribute to works by the writer Voltaire.

ZELDA

Novelist and diarist Zelda Fitzgerald (1900–1948) had a cat called Chat and two dogs, one named Ezra Pound and the other Bouillabaisse (otherwise known as Muddy Water or Jerry).

ZOLA

Novelist Emile Zola (1840–1902) had a black Pomeranian called Pinpin (full name, Chevalier Hector de Perlinpinpin). When Zola was accused of libel after his outspoken comments in the notorious Dreyfus case, the writer was forced to temporarily flee France in 1898 and settle in England. He had to leave his beloved Pinpin behind because of the UK's restrictions on bringing animals into the country, and Pinpin died shortly after Zola's departure.

The story goes that Pinpin, who used to sit with Zola, while he wrote, on his writing table or in his wastepaper basket, died of a broken heart. When he heard about Pinpin's death, Zola suffered an angina attack. Zola had a small graveyard for his pets (see also C is for cemetery) at his home in Médan to the north west of Paris on a small island on the Seine. Pinpin, and another favourite dog Fanfan, are both buried there.

ZWERG

Colette (1873–1954), author of the novellas *Gigi* and *La Chatte*, had dozens of cats including Franchette, Kiki-la-Doucette, La Chatte Dernière, La Touteu, Pinichette and Zwerg.

LIST OF ILLUSTRATIONS

All illustrations are from the collections of the British Library unless otherwise stated.

Page 45. Newfoundland. 'A Distinguished Member of the Humane Society', heliogravure of painting by Sir Edwin Landseer, 1876.

Page 47. Hare. Thomas Bewick, *A general history of Quadrupeds*, New York, 1804.

Page 48. Edward Lear and Foss, self-portrait by Edward Lear from a letter sent to William Latham Bevan, 1879. Add. 61891, f.110 (detail).

Page 50. Virginia Woolf, *Flush: a biography*, London, 1933.

Page 54. Edouard Manet, *Design for the poster and cover for 'The Raven' by Edgar Allan Poe*, lithograph, 1875. The Metropolitan Museum of Art, New York.

Page 56. Théophile Gautier, illustration by Nadar, *Journal Pour Rire, Journal Amusant*, 6 November 1858.

Page 61. Edouard Manet, *Perched Upon a Bust of Pallas,* Illustration for 'The Raven' by Edgar Allan Poe, lithograph, 1875. The Metropolitan Museum of Art, New York.

Page 64. Hare. Richard Brinsley Hinds, *The Zoology of the voyage of H.M.S. Sulphur*, London, 1843-45.

Page 68. Siamese. Paul Mégnin, *Notre ami le Chat*, Paris, 1899.

Page 69. The Domestic Cat. Thomas Bewick, *A general history of Quadrupeds*, Newcastle-upon-Tyne, 1807.

Page 70. Kittens. W.R. Stark, *A Book of Cats*, Toronto, 1921.

Page 74. Champfleury, *Les Chats. Histoire-moeurs-observations-anecdotes*, Paris, 1870.

Page 76. Brown tabby cat. Gordon Staples, *Cats, their points and characteristics*, London, 1876.

Page 80. Mastiff. Thomas Bewick, *A general history of Quadrupeds*, New York, 1804.

Page 83. Cornelis Visscher, *The Large Cat*, engraving, c.1657. British Museum, London.

Page 86. George Shaw, *The Zoology of New Holland*, London, 1794.

Page 88. 'M' is for mouse, Edward Lear, *Nonsense Botany, and Nonsense Alphabets*, London, 1889.

Page 92. Marmoset. Jules Trousset, *Nouveau Dictionnaire encyclopédique universel illustré*, Paris, 1884–86.

Page 98. Mongoose. Oliver Herford, *A Child's Primer of Natural History*, London, 1900.

Page 101. English Setter. W.R. Stark, *A Book of Dogs*, Toronto, 1921.

Page 102. Gottfried Mind, *Der Katzen-Raphael*, Berlin, 1861.

Page 106. Maltese. After Sir Edwin Landseer, *The Lion-Dog of Malta – The Last of His Tribe*, 1844. Metropolitan Museum of Art, New York.

Page 108. Edward Lear, *Nonsense Botany, and Nonsense Alphabets*, London, 1889.

Page 112. *The Illustrated Sporting and Dramatic News*, 5 February, 1876.

Page 114. Pekingese. *The Queen*, 19 October, 1889.

Page 115. Edward Lear, *Nonsense Botany, and Nonsense Alphabets*, London, 1889.

Page 118. Moriz Jung, *Greyhound*, colour lithograph, 1912. Metropolitan Museum of Art, New York.

Page 120. Oliver Herford, *Oliver Herford's Animal Book*, London, 1906.

Page 122. Collie. W.R. Stark, *A Book of Dogs*, Toronto, 1921.

Page 124. *Fables de Florian, illustrées par J.-J. Grandville*, Paris, 1842.

Page 126. Edward Lear and Foss, self-portrait by Edward Lear from a letter sent to William Latham Bevan, 1879. Add. 61891, f.110.

Page 128. Christina Rossetti, *The Children's Rossetti*, London, 1914.

Page 130. Chats de Siam. Paul Mégnin, *Notre ami le Chat*, Paris, 1899.

Page 132. Dalmatian. Cecil Aldin, *An Artist's models*, London, 1930.

Page 133. Christina Rossetti, *The Children's Rossetti*, London, 1914.

Page 135. Starling. Johann Andreas Naumann, *Naturgeschichte des Vögel Mittel-Europas*, Gera-Untermhaus, 1905.

Page 138. Edward Lear, *Nonsense Botany, and Nonsense Alphabets*, London, 1889.

Page 141. Victor Hugo's cat Chanoine. Champfleury, *Les Chats. Histoire-moeurs observations-anecdotes*, Paris, 1870.

Page 144. Cecil Aldin, *Dogs of Character*, London, 1927.

Page 145. Edwin Landseer, *A series of 17 engravings from drawings of animals*, London, 1848.

Page 146. Airedale Terrier. W.R. Stark, *A Book of Dogs*, Toronto, 1921.

Page 152. Dante Gabriel Rossetti lamenting the death of his Wombat. Pen and ink drawing by Rossetti, 1869. British Museum, London.

Page 154. Gottfried Mind, *Der Katzen-Raphael*, Berlin, 1861.

Page 155. Toto, illustration by Walter Denslow. L. Frank Baum, *The New Wizard of Oz*, Indianapolis, 1906.

156. Pomeranian. W.R. Stark, *A Book of Dogs*, Toronto, 1921.

Page 160. Illustration by Marguerite Kirmse to 'The Power of the Dog', Rudyard Kipling, *Collected Dog Stories*, London, 1934.